Political Theology and the Life of the Church

ANDRÉ DUMAS

Political Theology
and the
Life of the Church

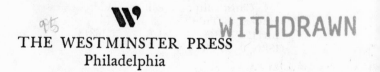

THE WESTMINSTER PRESS
Philadelphia

Translation by John Bowden from the French
Théologies Politiques et Vie de l'Eglise,
first published 1977 by Les Editions du Chalet, Lyon

Translation © John Bowden 1978

Published by The Westminster Press®
Philadelphia, Pennsylvania

PRINTED IN THE UNITED STATES OF AMERICA
9 8 7 6 5 4 3 2 1

Library of Congress Cataloging in Publication Data

Dumas, André.
  Political theology and the life of the church.

  Translation of Théologies politiques et vie de l'église.
  Bibliography: p.
  1. Christianity and politics — Addresses, essays,
lectures. I. Title.
  BR115.P7D813   261.7   78-16813
  ISBN 0-664-24226-X

Contents

Preface

This book began as a series of lectures which I gave in March 1976 as visiting professor of ecumenical studies at the Centre Unité chrétienne within the Faculty of Catholic Theology in the University of Lyons. What ecumenical Christianity seems to amount to these days is that all of us, within our different churches and outside them, are preoccupied with similar questions. How can I make use of the Bible in a contemporary political and social context without either manipulating it or leaving it out of account? Can I make any progress on the basis of theological conviction and political involvement without either giving up one in favour of the other or forcibly adjusting one to the other? How can I reconcile a quest for God and secular planning in a way which adds up to more than a vague combination of 'spiritual' aspirations with ideological affirmations, economic pressures and even tactical opportunities?

I would like to think that I could answer these three questions clearly, not so much by simply putting forward my own personal opinions as by inviting the reader to consider what might be a possible political theology, that is to say, a belief in God which regards him as a free and powerful Word with a beneficial effect on human society. I am doubtful, however, about the prospects of success here. In our pluralist, secular society there can be no question of a theocracy. How can we imagine the God of faith being used as an unchallengable source of legislation? Similarly, how can we imagine the existence of Christian parties, which would combine the word of the gospel with a

programme for the organization of society? That would mean
that those who belonged to such parties would become committed supporters rather than witnesses, and it would make
those who did not belong to them the objects of religious
suspicion or even of ecclesiastical condemnation. We should,
however, be realistic about the present situation: the risk of
theocracy is much less than the risk that the church may be
forced to the periphery of society. Middle-class views are
remarkably similar to Marxist ideology in this respect: religion
is still tolerable, and sometimes even useful, so long as it is a
private affair. I am not using 'private' here to denote a free
personal choice; it signifies the exclusion of religion in any form
from the sphere of public affairs. There is, in this view, a place
for both religion and politics, but religion belongs in its walled
garden and politics in the market place.

Contemporary political theologies have come into being as a
protest against this attempt to put religion on the sidelines. I
shall examine their ebb and flow over recent years and consider
what they have contributed and what they have failed to con-
tribute to the life of the church. I am well aware of the brevity
of the discussion and of the objections that might be made to it.
I shall be under fire from two directions. First there are those
who fear that the church may come under political influence,
in other words, those who are hesitant about the way in which
the Christian community all too often imitates the civil community and reproduces its divisions. Secondly, there are those
who feel that a detached approach – I would prefer to say
biblical and theological reflection – is one form or another of
idealism and tends to inhibit actual progress. Still, one should
not be so presumptuous as to expect to convince everyone. The
important thing is to be open to all points of view.

If I had to sum up the basic themes of the book in this
preface, I would single out two for special mention.

First of all, I have explored how as Christians we might live
with what I have rather pompously called a 'meta-textual'
approach. 'Meta-textual' is a play on words rather like the
ancient term 'metaphysics', the contemplative quest for an

eternity beyond time, matter and chance. There is also an echo of the modern term 'meta-history', in connection with which Marxism in particular is seen as a scientific method for recognizing and activating a quest to transform society, and indeed humanity. It indicates something beyond, in this case ahead of, the present period of alienation and exploitation. The history of the Christian community has been played out and continues to be played out in these two epochs. However, its fundamental characteristic is not to be found there. It is neither metaphysical nor meta-historical, but meta-textual. In the last of these three words 'meta' changes its meaning. It no longer signifies 'beyond', or 'in front of', but 'with'. How can we still live with the texts of the Old and New Testaments which are contingent, past, pluriform and hortatory? How are we to move to and fro between our time and theirs? How are we to find in their specific statements a realism which we cannot discover either in metaphysics or in meta-history? That is the first question. I have deliberately avoided those scholarly words which have now become so common: hermeneutics, interpretation, actualization and interrogation. I prefer to use simpler terminology and to talk about companionship and shared existence with the texts. However, I hope that I have not made light of the difficulties of developing an approach from them or watered down the promise of life in company with them.

The second theme has to do with the content of the texts. It seems to me that the Bible knows nothing of two great ideas which the Christian church has baptized as it were one after the other: the common good, so dear to metaphysical harmony, and the classless society, so dear to meta-historical expectation. Instead, the Bible recounts the story of a 'fratriarchy' in conflict. Like 'meta-textual', the term 'fratriarchy' also calls for some explanation. Once again it is a play on words, this time as a protest against patriarchy, which is supposed to be the human and the divine essence of the message of the Bible. The framework of the civilization within which the biblical authors lived may indeed have been essentially patriarchal, but the content of their message seems to me to be fratriarchal. 'Fratry' does not sound right because it is a technical term in ethnology, and 'brotherhood' is even less suitable, because it sounds too idealistic. So I have coined the word 'fratriarchy'. It comprises both conflict and reunion, if one comes to see the cross of Jesus Christ as the killing of a brother and his resurrection as a reunion with hostile brethren, as the renewal of the people of God on earth.

Thus the whole study is fashioned around two themes: a 'meta-textual' existence and a 'fratriarchal' history. Neither of these words can be found in a dictionary, and that disturbs me. After all, to paraphrase Descartes, theological language often becomes the least shared thing in the world. Lack of clarity has never led to profundity. So if you can, look on these two words as provocative word-plays to help us forward rather than as pretentious obscurantism.

I would like to express my thanks to Père Michalon, who invited me to Lyons, and to Père Roche, who welcomed me there. I would also like to say a special word of thanks to Père Pouts, the literary director of Editions du Chalet. He has been that thorn in my flesh without which an author continues to walk alone, because he has no brother for his text!

I

The Nature of Politics and the
Mission of the Church

Over recent years we have seen a revival of political theologies. That does not mean that theology has come under political influence, bringing with it the risk that theology will turn out to be a clerical seal of approval on a variety of options and analyses. Rather, it amounts to a stress on the political dimensions of theology, which are to be found throughout its range and which are capable of transformation. So it is not so much a matter of having God on our side in our personal or collective plans as of recognizing and living out the fact that God uses us on his side in *his* earthly struggles. This is why 'revolution' and 'liberation' often seem to be adequate and topical translations of 'conversion' and 'salvation'. However, as in any piece of translation, it is difficult to know whether the desire to refurbish an archaic word by finding a more modern equivalent may not be an act of treachery. We may seem to have preserved the original, but perhaps it may have lost its flavour in the process. At the same time, we have to compare politics, which need not necessarily be life according to the gospel, with the task of the church, which is not fundamentally a political enterprise. Since I do not wish to begin either by contrasting the church and politics or by making them seem too similar, I shall first consider the links between them and the way in which the various contemporary political theologies have made their appearance.

Three stages in modern theology

I shall distinguish three periods in the development of modern theology in order to indicate the context in which political theology arose.

The first covers the years between the First and Second World Wars. This was the period of theologies concerned with the transcendence of God and the eschatological coming of his Word into the world. They represent a break with the liberalism of nineteenth-century Protestant theology, which had a close parallel in modernism within the Roman Catholic church. The great difference here, of course, is that whereas modernism had been condemned by the Catholic authorities, liberalism had permeated Protestant culture. The liberals accepted that the critical judgment of history rules out all forms of dogmatism, including a dogmatism which affirms an eschatological revelation. By contrast, they saw the foundation of theology as being the inner experience of man's religious consciousness, believing that this was more authentic than any exaggerated and outward transcendence. The liberals thus had a critical respect for the facts of history, while remaining acutely sensitive to inner religious experience. By contrast, the theologies of the transcendent Word stressed the eschatological element of the coming of a God who is above and beyond history, above and beyond experience. Eschatology signifies that the last, central, ultimate moment really does come. History ceases to be judge and comes under judgment, and experience is no longer the source but the destination of the Word which comes from beyond.

In my formal outline, I would include both the dogmatism of Karl Barth and the exegesis of Rudolf Bultmann among these theologies of the Word, of the decisive eschatological event.

The essential characteristic of Barth seems to me to be the systematic way in which he develops a theology of revelation in which the divine Trinity accomplishes his plan of eternal election in Jesus Christ. Eschatology is the realization in time of a divine choice which has been made before all time. In his Son, the Christ, God accomplishes in the last times his eternal design of loving man and the world. In Christ we see the realization of the eschatology which is at the heart of history and the plenary presence of God in human experience.

Unlike Barth, Bultmann sees eschatology not so much from the perspective of God's eternal design and consequently in terms of his original election, as from the perspective of man and his existential choice. The approach of the Kingdom of God confronts man with an ultimate eschatological decision. The demythologization of the New Testament texts, which made Bultmann famous, was an attempt to put a readiness for the miraculous risk of faith, rather than a belief in miraculous events, at the heart of Christianity. So the idea of the decision of faith is as important for Bultmann as the idea of election by grace is for Barth. In either case this is a last, final moment in the sense in which Camus remarked, 'The last judgment takes place today.' Today, the instant of the existential decision by which I choose to believe or to harden my heart, is the moment when I realize that time is not simply a critical history or a period of indefinite duration but the unique eschatological opportunity. 'Today the kingdom of God has come upon you.' 'Today his eternal design of love is accomplished.'

Barth and Bultmann subsequently parted company. Barth accused Bultmann of reducing the objective revelation of the divine Trinity to an anthropocentric understanding of salvation, in which man's capacity to comprehend becomes the preliminary to and sometimes the yardstick of God's revelation. And Bultmann accused Barth of contributing to a revival of dogmatic orthodoxy which systematized the message of the Bible without taking account either of historical criticism or of the modern hearer's capacity for belief. In Barth's eyes, Bultmann limited faith too much to what modern man can believe, and in Bultmann's eyes, Barth tied faith too much to what men should always believe. At this point, however, I am not concerned to describe their progressive estrangement, but rather to recall their common and fundamental origin.

In breaking with liberalism and its inner religious consciousness, Barth and Bultmann both stressed the transcendence of

God. He comes down to us from above, for us, among us. He is an eschatological event, a Word that is ultimate and present, unforeseeable and decisive, which we have no way of producing from deep within ourselves unless God comes and speaks. In contrast to the timelessness of religious and moral consciousness, in contrast to the remembrance of a forgotten depth, in contrast to the idealism of a quest for the ultimate, Barth and Bultmann are both theologians of the eschatological Word realized in Jesus Christ.

To underline their affinity, let me quote two phrases from this same period: 'The situation on Sunday morning is related in the most literal sense to the end of history; it is eschatological, even from the viewpoint of the people, quite apart from the Bible. That is to say, when this situation arises, history, further history, is done with, and the ultimate desire of man, the desire for an ultimate event, now becomes authoritative.'[1] 'The Kingdom of God determines the present because it now compels man to decision; he is determined thereby either in this direction or in that, as chosen or as rejected, in his entire present existence.'[2] For anyone who did not know the sources, the quotation from Barth might well appear Bultmannian and that from Bultmann Barthian!

These two theologies of the Word, the Word of God's election and the Word which constitutes man in the fundamental decision of his faith, are characteristic of what I have called theologies of transcendence, of the coming of the Word and of realized eschatology.

At the end of the last war a second period followed which saw the development of hermeneutical theologies, i.e. theologies concerned with the interpretation of language. In this connection one might mention the names of a French and of a German author, Gerhard Ebeling and Paul Ricoeur;[3] the influence of the 'second' Heidegger is present in the background. This is not the 'first' Heidegger with his existentialist view of man 'thrown into the world' and called upon to make a decision in the face of death, but the 'second' Heidegger, who sees language as the expression of Being, which underlies it, in a way which is present and yet hidden. From now on the profundity of language takes the place of the transcendent Word as the way towards God. Interpretation, in Greek hermeneutics, is an attempt to listen to the Word, taking account of the fact that it comes to us through texts from the past and through language in the present.

Texts have an objective existence apart from us, but if we allow ourselves to be challenged or, more precisely, interpreted by them, they become our masters. This second period was one of creative encounter between contemporary existence and the texts, since to interpret is not simply to know but actually to understand, in the precise sense of the word, i.e. to 'stand under' the texts and allow them to be themselves. Here the encounter is no longer between man and the transcendent Word, but between human existence and language, seen as a setting and its decipherment.

This second period of hermeneutical theologies was more sensitive than that of the theologies of the Word to all the problems raised by the distance between ourselves and God. God's witness comes to us by means of texts. Since these texts belong to a time different from our own, we have to make transpositions in order to overcome their remoteness without forgetting their particular emphasis. Reflection on the interpretation which proves inevitable and indispensable now replaces claims about revelation and realized eschatology, which were common in the previous period.

About ten years ago, we entered a third period with the development of political theologies. To illustrate this third period, I shall mention three names: Jürgen Moltmann, Wolfhart Pannenberg and Jean-Baptiste Metz. [4]

How are we to describe these political theologies, coming as they do after theologies of the Word (concerned with transcendence) and hermeneutical theologies (concerned with interpretation)?

First of all, it is typical of these political theologies that they have rediscovered the importance of the book of Revelation, the Apocalypse. It is the word 'apocalyptic', rather than 'eschatological', which gives them their particular colouring, though in fact apocalyptic was formerly seen as an expression of religious culture in the time of Jesus. Its language was thought to be both anachronistic, since we no longer share this fervent expectation of the end of our world, and mistaken, since what came next was not the kingdom and the transformation of the earth, but the resurrection and the formation of the church. By and large, therefore, theologies of transcendence and hermeneutical theologies make a contrast between eschatology, which is a matter of decision, and apocalyptic, which is time-conditioned.

For example, Bultmann thought that apocalyptic was a cultural language borrowed by the New Testament from contemporary Judaism. Legalism, apocalyptic and gnosticism were the false friends from which the message of the New Testament had to be detached. He thought that to retain its language, characteristic of Judaism in the time of Jesus, was to be trapped in an obsolete cultural mould. Instead of presenting the central Christian message of free justification by grace, it expressed useless anxiety over a parousia which had not been realized, an imminent return of Jesus Christ which had not come about. Bultmann thus devalued apocalyptic, seeing it as a transitory mode of expression, a clumsy mythological garb for the central message of eschatology, that with Jesus Christ the end-time had come. The true message of the gospel, then, was not to be confused with the apocalyptic fever which was so prominent in the New Testament environment. The preaching of the apostles set out to reduce the emotional temperature by centring the faith of the growing church on the cross and resurrection of Jesus Christ, rather than on speculations about the immediate outcome of history.

In the same way, the majority of classical Christian writers were very cautious about the theme of apocalyptic, which brings with it the risk that faith in Christ may be turned into curiosity about the future. Most of the great historical churches have regarded apocalyptic fervour as a matter of marginal concern. For example, Luther refused to write a commentary on the Apocalypse, leaving it, one might say, to the left wing of Christianity. The left wing was interested in revolution in this world, whereas the classical churches proclaimed how God's plan had been accomplished in the cross and resurrection of Christ.

All contemporary political theologies have had second thoughts about apocalyptic. They have understood it as an affirmation that history still has something new in store, a future which has not been fully realized in the first coming of Jesus Christ. This first coming was the realization of reconciliation through him. However, reconciliation will be followed by redemption. Before us and still to come is God's future. (Moltmann makes much of this, playing on the construction of the German word *Zukunft* = 'to come'.) History carries within itself an expectation of fulfilment at the level of its messianic promise.

So Christianity has not abandoned messianic expectations. Christianity can arouse messianic expectations as well as Judaism. The mistake of the churches was to suppress them in favour of an emphasis on what Christ had accomplished on earth. It is, however, characteristic of Christianity that it does not deaden expectation but quickens it. Messianic hope is renewed, prompted by the belief that the first coming of Jesus Christ must be followed by a second coming which lies ahead. So Christian faith has a great affinity to Jewish thought. Hope remains a fundamental category which is neither suppressed nor diminished by faith. On the contrary, faith quickens hope. Faith increases and deepens expectation. The 'not yet' felt by those who hope is nourished by belief in what is 'already there'.

The first characteristic of political theologies, then, is to insist more on apocalyptic than eschatology. The theologies of the Word deal with an eschatological fulfilment which has already taken place: in the end-time of Christ and in our faith today. By contrast, political theologies are revivals of an apocalyptic view focussed on what has yet to take place in the history of the world and concentrating human energy in that direction.

Let me add a second comment, though I am well aware how Ecclesiastes mocks those who believe themselves to be innovators.[5] Whereas earlier theologies were concerned with personal conversion, political theologies emphasize the collective dimensions of life. In this sense, too, they are apocalyptic. The Apocalypse is full of crowds, great gatherings which recapitulate the twelve tribes of the Old Testament and the twelve apostles of the New. It is also a book about collective achievements. All that has been hinted at, announced, lived out beforehand in the lives of individuals is now summed up and repeated in a final collective recapitulation. Thus, to take a classic example, the Apocalypse speaks of a general resurrection at the end of history, instead of being preoccupied with the personal salvation of each individual immediately after his own death. It describes the collective future of a humanity in terms of two cities: mankind as a whole is raised with Jerusalem and submerged with Babylon. Political theologies use collective categories like those to be found in apocalyptic, whereas theologies of the Word or hermeneutical theologies speak more of the existential and personal decision provoked by eschatology, even if Barth was obviously more political than Bultmann or Ebeling. Thus 'political' theology comprises not only messianic expectations for earthly history, but also collective thought and practice.

Finally, political theologies have begun in a very optimistic way, as though the resurrection held out a prospect of nothing but the hope of victory. Indeed, this tendency was taken so far that subsequently the ardour stemming from the Easter transformation had to be tempered by a remembrance of the suffering and the realism of the cross. These theologies draw pictures of tomorrows which already contain the beginnings of a recapitulation, liberation and universalization of the experience of all mankind. Their vision of the Trinity is resolutely 'economic',[6] if it is possible at this point to distinguish the 'economic' from the 'immanent' Trinity. The immanent Trinity is the continual presence of the three persons, Father, Son and Holy Spirit, in the inner communion of God. It is the affirmation of the eternal coexistence of the three persons and therefore, to borrow a phrase from Marcuse, of the tridimensional character of God throughout time. The economic Trinity is centred more on the unfolding of the history of salvation: first the Father reigns, then the Son, and finally, as a new development, the Spirit. The economic Trinity is a concept which suggests that the future has an effect on God; it influences not only man's knowledge of God but sometimes even God's very being. How does God develop through the different stages which he goes through with humanity?

Such an understanding of a God who develops progressively through his involvement in earthly history perhaps derives from the pneumatological enthusiasm of Joachim of Fiore in the Middle Ages; it certainly owes much to the influence of Hegel's philosophy. It was Hegel who gave God this place in the future of the world. First there is the Father, an abstract and solitary totality, a being who remains by himself, absolute and inaccessible, in the form of a universal abstraction. Then there is the Son, as Hegel describes him: concrete and particular. By him the Father comes forth from himself, enters the world in the incarnation, and dies with the world in the cross. Here, then, the cross is not in essence a catastrophic consequence of man's sin; it is the conclusion of a process to which the powers of darkness cannot put a stop, the mysterious and miraculous abolition of the difference between God and the world. God becomes the world, flesh and death without ceasing to be God, in this incarnation by which his divine being takes concrete form, shedding light on a speculative Good Friday. Thus the Son is the open door to the Spirit, the universal in concrete form. From now on this universal can extend out into a world in which its triumphant outpouring brings an end to all divisions, which beforehand were unfortunate but necessary. The reign of the Spirit is the entry of God into the variegated totality of the world and the involvement of the totality of the world in the one great reconciliation of God.

Such a vision of the progress of the Trinity provides political theologies with both a messianic expectation which is optimistic about the future of history and a historical confidence in the future of theology. Theology is not so much an eschatological judgment on history or an interpretation of our lives arising out of work on texts as the progress of a specific hope in expectation of the fulfilment of the Trinity. It remains to be seen whether at this point Hegel's philosophy of history does not often get the better of the proclamation of salvation in Jesus Christ.

I might also add that, at least to begin with, political theologies have shown signs of more optimistic assurance (perhaps because of their foundation in trinitarian speculation) than Marxism. The latter has a somewhat utopian vision of the decisive juncture which, at some moment or other, will mark the passage from prehistory to history. History will be the communist society, a society which has yet to be achieved anywhere. The transition remains a utopian expectation, even if Marxism claims to have a scientific approach. Political theologies are also much more optimistic than the social phenomenology of Sartre in his *Critique de la Raison Dialectique*. Here, in a first stage, individuals exist side by side in 'series'; in a second stage they 'fuse' in a creative upsurge of freedom. However, the third stage is a regression, in which the group is preserved by taking an institutional form. The 'series' develops towards the 'fusion', but then lapses into becoming an institution. This is no longer the Hegelian vision of synthesis and achievement, but the 'leftist' vision, with its mistrust of institutions and their enclosed character. It is a vision of transitory messianic moments, lacking that ultimate apocalyptic optimism which is to be found, by contrast, in political theologies.

As a result, by virtue of their apocalyptic aspect, which points to a future realization and recapitulation, these theologies proclaim a corporate consummation. Unlike the theologies of the Word and hermeneutical theologies, they do not just describe an encounter either in the advent of transcendence or in the depths of language. Contemporary Christianity needs these political theologies to affirm the collective and historical dimensions of a messianic perspective which has been revived by the coming of Jesus Christ, if the Apocalypse is to regain its relevance for our world. Political theologies are critical of a society which is anxious for preservation without future expectations, and of a church which provides justification and legitimation without any thought of conversion or transformation. The church has, in fact, always had a political horizon, long before political theologies became the present fashion.

Politics, a necessary dimension of the life of the church

Since it has been called together and raised up by a universal God, the church is inevitably involved in politics, if politics amounts to a concern for the active coexistence of all men. The real reason why the church cannot avoid the world of politics is that it does not simply propagate a particular religion which is a private possibility for individuals. From a sociological perspective the church may be a minority, but theologically speaking it seeks to address the whole world. Israel's God calls himself the God of all the earth, and Jesus Christ comes as bread for the whole world. The Israelites were surrounded by super-powers which from a historical point of view were far more important, but they were nevertheless reminded that their God, Yahweh, was Lord of heaven and earth. They were the only people to know the proper name of Yahweh, but their God was more than just their God. He was also the God of Egypt, of Assyria and of Persia, the God of the islands at the ends of the earth. The Israelites called God by his name, but that did not make Yahweh their own national God. There is a great tension in the Old Testament because it attests a special revelation but does not lay exclusive claim to it: on the contrary, God often has better servants outside Israel than within!

It is therefore imperative that the church should retain a political dimension in its message if faith in Jesus Christ is not to be considered merely a matter of opinion. It cannot just be a private religion, tolerated by, or a matter of indifference to, certain citizens and with no real significance for society as a whole. It is remarkable that the middle classes and the Marxists are agreed in seeing religion as a private affair; their view

seems to derive from what is often a legitimate reaction against a
clerical domination of secular control which the church has
misguidedly sought to exercise or to prolong. However, while
we must reject clerical manipulation, it is equally important to
withstand any attempt to make Christianity a matter of
marginal concern and to relegate it to the private sphere. This
need has been clear since the beginning of Christianity, from
the time when Christians were only a tiny minority. The great
political concern of the New Testament was to warn the church
against being tempted by this minority situation or being
content with it. Should that happen, the church would remain
a sect, if one understands a sect to be a group which feels
society to be corrupt, lost and of no account, and therefore sets
out to lead a life of its own. A sect like this has no concern for
the political future of the world. It breaks away and goes into
retreat. By contrast the church, even if it is a minority, is
involved with all men and puts its challenge to them. This
seems to be the sense of the famous thirteenth chapter of
Romans, which appears between other chapters dealing with
private and interpersonal relationships. It does more than
provide a theological foundation for the state. For there are
two great dimensions to Christian existence, and one does not
rule out the other.

Relationships are formal when we know people only by
name; they become close and emotional with those nearer to
us, where affection plays an enormous part and both discretion
and generosity are important. We corrupt our private lives if
we break confidences or disclose shared intimacies. In such
cases publicity becomes a destructive kind of 'voyeurism'.
There is no need to divulge to the whole world personal secrets
that we may have uncovered. If the private domain is absorbed
into the political sphere, there is a risk that what is meant to
be an exchange of confidences between two people will be
proclaimed to the whole world.

There is, however, a second sphere, that of politics, which is
just as important, but is less capable of being absorbed than the
first. The political sphere involves dealings with unknown

people with whom we are associated by cold impersonal institutions rather than by warm emotions. There we are no more than numbers, part of the organization, without personal relationships in which we call one another by name. At times we may be involved in organizational relationships; in series and structures, groups and political entities. Political relationships are by nature anonymous, cold, structured and public. Politics ought, as far as possible, to be carried on in public. Politics is corrupted by secrecy in the same way as private relationships are corrupted by exhibitionism. As soon as politics is manipulated in a clandestine fashion, secretly and undemocratically, as soon as it is at the mercy of personal influence and personal relationships, it is corrupted and becomes crypto-authoritarian.

If, then, there are two great dimensions to life, the church should not confine itself to one or the other. When the church moves to the periphery of society, over-reacting in contrition for its former attitude of clerical triumphalism, its great temptation is to settle for the realm of personal relationships and to leave organized society outside its sphere of competence and its mission. In that case, the church becomes an oasis or a ghetto, and ceases to proclaim the God of all the earth. Present-day political theologies are rediscovering that human life has other dimensions, public as well as private; politics involves structures and organizations. However, this rediscovery does not suggest that the personal realm must be eliminated, or absorbed into the wider social sphere. To do this would be to distort the character of private life, just as we distort it when we forget that it extends into politics. Thus the church has to concern itself with both dimensions of life, and political theologies are required to rescue Christianity from an exclusive concentration on private life.

Having said all this, we should recognize that the relationship between the church and politics is a difficult one.

First of all, there is a technical difficulty. What are the respective spheres of competence of the church and politics? During the era of Christendom, the church thought that the whole of society came within its sphere of competence and under its control. In modern times the church can see how many other independent authorities are aware of the complexity of the problems involved and have some control over the interplay of forces. When it lacks this awareness or this control, the church feels reduced to making moralistic generalizations or ineffective statements. Sheer ignorance of the complexity of the problems involved drives it to make moralistic pronouncements without spiritual content. A spiritual pronouncement has force in a particular context. A moralistic pronouncement – in the pejorative sense – simply expresses a pious hope. It gives no specific indication of what is to happen as a result, nor does it go into the specific decisions which will have to be taken if anything is to come of it. It is worth recalling that Jesus did not consider that he was competent in every respect. For example, he refused to pass judgment in a dispute over an inheritance: 'Man, who made me a judge or divider over you?' (Luke 12.14). Thus if the gospel has a central sphere of competence, the proclamation of forgiveness, by contrast at its periphery there will be a series of mundane questions about which the church may not feel that it has anything to say. This is because it has to leave discussion on such questions to others. However, it should be noted that the passage from Luke which I have quoted does lead on to a discussion of the problem of covetousness and the desire to seek security in possessions. So the fact that the church has no competence in this sphere cannot be made an excuse for forgetting its spiritual competence.

The second difficulty is much more serious. The message of the gospel is a radical one. How can it have any practical effect if this radical character is maintained? As we listen to the Sermon on the Mount and remember how it was fulfilled in the crucifixion of Jesus, the message of the gospel seems to be that God renounces his rights so that guilty men may live and not be condemned. Its central theme is that God waives his right to retribution in order to justify the guilty by an act of regeneration which seems quite scandalous. The heart of the gospel, then, is the justification of the sinner, when to exercise retributive justice would demand his condemnation. But what political application can there be for a message about waiving one's rights in favour of the guilty party? On the contrary, politics is a matter of maintaining, defending, competing for rights which are exercised by one side and claimed by another. So how can we find any kind of catalyst for the political struggle in the gospel?

Nietzsche expressed his doubts about this in two ways. First, he saw the gospel as the outcome of the resentment of feeble men who were incapable of exercising their rights by force and therefore projected their weakness in spite and vengeance. They claimed that to renounce one's rights was the summit of human behaviour. For Nietzsche, the gospel is not the proclamation of justification by grace for sinners; it stems from the envy of the weak, who have renounced their rights because they are incapable of exercising them. The gospel is a sub-conscious expression of impotence rather than the sovereign proclamation of grace. According to Nietzsche, Christianity does not derive from the fulfilment of the promise made freely to Abraham, but from a pathetic rebellion on the part of people of no account. The gospel is not the justification of the poor but a shameful accusation made by the weak.

Nietzsche's second theme is strangely bound up with the first. In contrast to St Paul, he thinks that Jesus envisaged the collapse of all existing orders: the family, the nation, the working world. He sees this collapse partly in eschatological terms, partly as an element in a game. According to Nietzsche, the Christianity of Jesus consists in the disestablishment of the earth and the overthrow of all institutions and all structures. Christianity, therefore, can be lived out only as part of the joyful and tragic game of life; it can never take the form of a political or ecclesiastical institution. That is why he argued that the church brought about the opposite of what Jesus wanted and proclaimed. I do not propose to discuss Nietzsche's interpretation here, or to go into his radical contrast between Jesus and Paul. But it is important to remember the difficulty he raised. How do we find in the gospel an inspiration which can be applied directly to politics? The question remains even if we reject the view that the gospel is vengeance taken by the powerless on those who have power and exercise political control, or that it is utterly unrelated to and has no concern for the responsibilities of the state and its institutions, taking both these as collective political dimensions that make up a human existence which goes beyond private and interpersonal relationships.

First, we saw the pressing need that the church should have a political horizon if it is to serve the God of all the earth. Now we have also seen the formidable dangers it faces when it speaks and acts politically: the danger of making moralistic judgments in areas outside its competence and the danger of being thought to be envious, bitter, or quite simply irresponsible.

The paradoxes of politics

However, politics itself is not in fact what it claims to be, either. Politics is full of contortions, and its claims are often false.[7] Politics is in theory universal and rational. It sets out to discover and formulate a worthwhile programme, to achieve an aim which is not deflected by whims and caprices, but based on a sure foundation. At one time this foundation will have been the validity of political regimes; today it is the validity of economic organizations. Politics thus seeks to involve all society in a rational process of education. The theme is an ancient one, going back as it does to a Platonism which is not escapism into the realm of ideas, but a realistic consideration of what ideas might form a basis for the education of 'the City'. Plato was concerned with what the City ought to be, not what it is. There is always a good deal of Platonism in contemporary political theory, which is developed in order to give a scientific structure to practical politics.

Politics may set out to be a necessary and rational business, but in practice it is marked by a good deal of emotional involvement. As political events develop, one can see politicians having an emotive preference for one value or another. The plurality of values and the way in which the choice of a particular value is affected by emotion undermines the claim of any political approach to be rational and necessary. It would be much more honest if there were an acknowledgment of the emotive preference underlying any political programme instead of the tendency of such political programmes to set themselves up as the only possible view to emerge from an objective analysis of the facts. At this point I am not at all concerned with self-interest, but simply with emotive preferences of any kind. Such emotional attachments to particular values, leading to the predominance of the value concerned, are crucial. In the end they affect the choice of the political programme which they advocate even more than its presentation, which claims to be rational and universal.

Likewise, politics always seeks to appear as the corporate administration of people and things. It presents itself as the most just and most hopeful way of managing human society. However, this claim to be the best form of administration also conceals a lust for power. Effective government certainly calls for power, but power is also intoxicating and benefits those who exercise it. Power is conquest, because politics remains a conflict between different groups. It involves conquest for the sake of gain and conquest to prevent the possibility of manipulation. Politicians fight to remain in power, claiming that they are only trying to remain in a position in which they can continue with effective government.

Here we come up against the first paradox of political life. Politics is presented as a rational solution, but in reality it is a matter of emotional preferences, the struggle for power and the concern to retain it. Its outward and reassuring aspect is its claim to rationality and universality, what is called in modern parlance its scientific theory. Its hidden face is the struggle to acquire power, sometimes through elections, sometimes through intrigues over succession.

That is why politics is always waged like a war, for all its claim to be concerned with peace. The relationship between its peaceful aspect and the aggressiveness of its way of going about things remains constant. Politics aims at a popular consensus and economic expertise. It seeks to bring about a society in which major conflicts are replaced by general agreements, with the aim of establishing peace within society for a certain period, at least in those areas where the state is involved. Nevertheless, both in wartime and in periods between wars, progress in this direction remains a belligerent affair, a series of confrontations. Power, then, is presented on the pretext of being a means to peace, whereas its use in politics involves a constant conflict. Being involved in politics is not just a matter of making rational or moral statements; it is also a matter of adding up the forces at one's disposal.

There is a second hidden paradox in politics. Politics is always presented as the means of realizing a programme. The ambition of politicians is to carry out a certain number of projects which they do not want to leave in the realm of ideas; these projects must take an institutional form or an ideological dimension. For ideology (in the positive sense of the word, not the distorted visage which has become so familiar) is a way of establishing a hold on the masses so that they will accept a particular institutional form. Politicians, then, state the programme they seek to carry out in a way calculated to unite the conformists and the militants. However, this public programme conceals unacknowledged interests and ambitions. Ambitions need not be harmful, because they represent a tendency to be found in all politics, and indeed in every enterprise. One has to choose between growth or decline: there is no way of standing still. Ambition provides an indispensable source of vitality. The trouble is that instead of allowing itself to be seen as a force, it is also capable of presenting itself as a fair view of the facts. It is prepared to lie in order to survive, and this lie gradually destroys the confidence that it seeks to build up. Finally, there are even more limiting factors than ambitions. Perhaps there is the need to win popular support; there may be economic pressures which narrow down the range of possible political choices. Thus whereas political programmes claim to be ideal, in fact they are under considerable pressure; hence the tension in any political regime between the splendour of the promise and the limited range of practical possibilities.

One last paradox. Politics presents history as a course of events that can be influenced, and not as a destiny. It is not content to bow to the future of the world but seeks to influence it, to bring the authority of the will to bear in order to change situations. This can happen through the appearance of a personality who can shape the future of history if he succeeds in transforming his inner visions into a force which influences the masses. However, such a development can be found, above all, in a capacity to accelerate and resolve the actual movements of history, so that it does not proceed towards an unhappy day of reckoning but towards an outcome which has yet to be realized. So politics aims to fertilize a hidden seed, to secure the future of a promising beginning which is menaced by injustice and human laziness. In this context, the positive element is the will of the individual which works against a sense of fatalism to summon up flagging energies and forge them into a common sense of purpose and to accelerate the course of history in order to bring its fragile hopes to birth.

The paradox arises from the fact that politics, which has the appearance of a personal concern or a science of necessary progress, often proves to be a question of reacting to unforeseen circumstances. Politics is a chance affair, a matter of opportunism rather than deliberate planning. In general, political events develop through seizing opportunities. Wars have created conditions in which socialist societies can develop. Revolutions have enabled great personalities to take the stage. But for unforeseen circumstances, breakdowns and opportunities, political thinking would never lead to political action. We would certainly have a Karl Marx, but not a Lenin! Even if politics claims to be a matter of individual concern or universal law, it only comes to something when chance opportunities are seized by spectators who suddenly decide to become actors.

Finally, politics is a quest for popular involvement in decision making which has been made possible by the initiative of an individual. It is the degree of popular support provided by a group which allows itself to be roused from its inertia and its illusions in order to take positive steps towards its destiny.

But who makes the decision here? At this point we are confronted with the two poles of political life: popular support and decision-making. It is important for the people to take a certain number of decisions so that they cease to be a mass and develop a conscience and a corporate sense. If there is popular involvement without the power to make decisions, politics tends to become a great morass, a tangle of communications and indecisive influences. There is agitation without any clear sense of direction; opinions are asked but there is no master plan; sails are trimmed to the prevailing wind. On the other hand, however, if decisions are made without participation, 'tyranny' (in the old Greek sense of the word) is never far away, even if it is tempered by democratic procedures. As a result, and here we come to the ultimate paradox, politics is the most corporate form of decision-making possible, or the least indecisive exchange of opinions that can be achieved: in other words, a democracy which is clear about the difficulty of proposing without imposing and deliberating without equivocation. In this sense, politics itself cherishes a utopian vision, if utopia is the combination of two apparently antagonistic values, liberty and community.

So it is not only the gospel that proves to be impracticable. Politics presents the same problem. A good political theology does not consist either in watering down the gospel or in idealizing politics. Each needs to help the other to incarnate the gospel, rather than reducing it to an impotent idealism, and to demystify politics, rather than making it into a false gospel.

Three situations of the church

Let me end these preliminary remarks with one last observation. The church is always at the mercy of circumstances. We are born in a century we did not choose. We live in a church that we did not make for ourselves. We are in an environment which does not belong to us. Those are the fundamental conditions not only of our own life but also of the incarnation. Jesus lived in a situation dominated by implacable hostility, and the church has no better lodging place than its master. Consequently, depending on the particular period, the church can find itself in three different political situations. It can be a 'state church', in which the civil community and the Christian community have common interests and stand shoulder to shoulder. A distinction is made between spiritual authority and temporal power, but in essence the one supports the other. The church backs the authorities in their role of government and pacification. The authorities protect and help the church in its spiritual task. The advantage is clear: the exercise of political power is at the centre of Christian concern. The church is not utterly indifferent to what becomes of society, as it is shaped by political power. However, the risk is even more evident: Caesaro-papism, clericalism, state religion, improper concordats, discrimination against citizens who profess a 'second-class' religion. In short, there is a temptation for the church to use political power to gain for itself, *qua* church, privileges which conflict with its mission of critical and disinterested service.

Secondly, the church can be a free church. In that case there is a separation between the churches and the civil power. This can amount to a favoured tolerance, sometimes just a veneer, at others a matter of complete indifference. In any event, the two authorities are completely separated. Here again the advantage is clear: clericalism is no longer a temptation for the church: temporal power is obviously a matter for the laity. All those who are not Christians can lead a full life in civil society. Faith becomes more clearly a free decision; there is no pressure, and it carries no advantages. Here, too, however, there is a hidden danger, that of marginalism. The church expresses a private opinion, which gains more respect the more discreet it is. In this case the corporate and political dimension of the Christian message can disappear as an incongruous element which disturbs the civil peace. The church has to be content to be a setting for private relationships among its members, which have no bearing on the political dimensions of their life.

Finally, the church may feel obliged to become a confessing church. Perhaps it may be actively persecuted, perhaps its administration may be compromised. There may be a desire to see it disappear from a particular society where its message seems pernicious or obsolete. Here again the advantage is clear: such a situation is a reminder that Christian existence is not favoured; on the contrary, Christians are challenged and harried, as they were not only in the beginning but so often during their history. We should not forget that other churches were involved in such persecution, not necessarily for religious reasons but because they wished to maintain their mono- polistic position as state churches. Faith is not insignificant, because it is contested. Christianity once again becomes a confession, whereas formerly it was a matter of conformity or tolerance. Here too, however, there is no less of a risk. This is without doubt the temptation towards millenarianism or apocalypticism. People become preoccupied with the kingdom which will come soon. They are completely disinterested in present-day politics.

I have described three typical situations. We cannot choose our own situation from them. Each has its advantages, and each conceals a difficulty.

The mission of the church differs, depending on the situation in which it finds itself. The worst thing that can happen is for a church to dream of a situation other than that in which it has been incarnated. For example, a free church should not behave as though it still had the authority of a state church or as if it longed for the rude awakening of the confessing church. However, if we are agreed that the greatest threat to a free church in our present situation is to be pushed aside and ren- dered insignificant, we shall try to discover how contemporary political theologies can assure such a church that politics is part of the gospel and assure civil society that the church is not seeking either to regain the standing of a state church or artificially to provoke the situation of a confessing church. As we have seen, politics itself is a field where the wheat of corporate concern is mixed with the tares of solitary power. Politics is as paradoxical, indeed as sick, as the other sectors of human existence. The church's mission is neither to condemn nor to hallow, but cure. 'Those who are well have no need of a physician, but those who are sick; I came not to call the righteous, but sinners' (Mark 2.17). This realistic acknowledgment of grace, which revives flagging energies, and of sin, which dispels illusions, makes it seem advantageous for the church always to be involved in politics, and for politicians to welcome the freedom introduced by the church of Jesus Christ, who became a servant in order to be freely recognized as the Lord of all our human lives.

2

Biblical Foundations in the
Prophets and Apostles

It is obviously impossible to construct a political theology on biblical principles, because the Bible does not contain any principles. It is the story of men at grips with the promises and the commandments of God. Still less can one construct a political theology on the basis of real-life situations, since human situations do not in themselves convey truth and need to be set in the context of the light which comes from God. We can, however, consider and seek to understand the direct encounter between the will of God and human politics which can already be found within the Bible. It is therefore clear that a political theology which looks for a biblical basis has to take account of the confrontations, the problems and the choices illustrated by the encounter of the witnesses of the Old and New Testaments with divine interventions. These did not give them anything to cling to, nor abandon them completely, but simply made them witnesses.

Revolution and restraint

I have decided to draw attention to the many stories of rival brothers within the Old Testament as a political model for revolution and to use the sense of a life lived in dependence on Jesus Christ which can be found in the New Testament as a model for political behaviour in the face of social restraint. Politics in fact moves between the two poles of revolution and restraint; it is not content with accepting the *status quo* and regarding it as divine providence, still less with denying it and dreaming of something quite different. Conservatism is resignation (or privilege. . .) disguised as wisdom. Revolution is negation (or irresponsibility) dressed up as justice. Both often amount to an evasion of political choice. The Old Testament prophets seem above all to be opposed to conservatism, constantly calling for a revolution which will restore human freedom, equality and brotherhood, whereas the apostles of the New Testament are predominantly against revolution, calling on men to accept social restraint in company with Jesus Christ, whose faithfulness to God's politics and whose fight against human opposition brought him to the cross. Paradoxically, one might argue that when it comes to providing biblical foundations for a political theology, the Old Testament seems the more revolutionary, and the New Testament the more conservative. However, we must go beyond such superficial generalizations. We need to investigate in more detail how the prophets struggle against the unjust division of society, whereas the apostles struggle to convey how new the faith is, even where social restraints persist. Hence, 'built upon the foundation of the apostles and prophets, Christ Jesus himself being the chief corner-stone' (Eph. 2.20), Christians can find enlightenment by means of two basic models of political life. 'Surrounded by these witnesses' (Heb. 12.1), we are left to go our own way, since life in faith is not a matter of retracing steps, nor of wandering off anywhere; it is companionship in freedom.

The fratriarchal relationship

My first theme is that of the fortunes of the fratriarchy in the Old Testament, the origin and rediscovery of human brotherhood according to the prophets of Israel. (I use 'prophet' here in the Jewish sense, so that it includes the historical books as well as those that we call prophetic.) The Old Testament stories may be set and narrated in a patriarchal form of civilization, but their basis, their substance and their message concerns the fratriarchy and not the patriarchy. What were the fortunes of brothers belonging to the same political grouping? In this context the word 'revolution' signifies a capacity to remedy a spoilt situation.

Old Testament man is essentially a social being.[8] The ancient Greek is also dependent on the group to which he belongs: he is a tragic hero who sees the ties of family and heredity as his destiny; a pupil of the philosophers, who sees the achievements of the institutions of the city state as his liberty. So he is never just an individual, without ancestors and without a city. However, if the ancient Greek has tragic determinacy or philosophical education as his destiny, his ideal is personal autonomy. Born in bonds, he looks for independence. Old Testament man has just the opposite characteristics: menaced by isolation, he realizes his full vocation in the rediscovery, recognition and confession of his dependence on others. We know that the addition of 'brotherhood' to 'equality' and 'liberty' on the banners of the French Revolution was a late development.[9] The ideal republican of the Greek city provided the first two revolutionary attributes, but the third was inspired by the history of a fratriarchy, which according to the Old Testament had to be reformed again and again.

According to the prophetic books, then, man has no existence apart from the various groups within which he lives out all the dimensions of his personal life. He is neither an individual, remote, feeble and solitary, nor is he an interchangeable number, lost and anonymous among the masses. He always represents the group of which he is a part, to such a degree that all of his actions are significant for the political life of the group. These actions may be individual acts of courage, like Abraham's acceptance of his call and his readiness to sacrifice Isaac, or Jacob's struggle with the angel at the ford of Jabbok, or they may be hidden and shameful, like Achan's crime against the law of the ban. Each individual act affects the destiny of the whole people, involves them in a breach of faith or loses them in the toils of confusion. Every man represents all his fellow human beings, in accordance with the clear-sighted laws of a solidarity watched over by God himself. But if each individual represents the whole people, he also profits from this solidarity, which brings not so much the sense of constant surveillance as that of a comforting companionship. That is why the Old Testament story is more one of dramatic episodes in the history of a fratriarchy than of the tragic consequences of a disastrous patriarchy.

An episode in the book of Joshua (7.16–18) will give us a better idea of the various representative groups to which an Israelite might belong. These groups are compromised by his individual action and at the same time represent his personal existence. The situation is that after the capture of Jericho someone has disobeyed the law of the ban by taking some of the spoil, which by rights belongs only to God. This culprit has to be found. 'So Joshua rose early in the morning, and brought Israel near tribe by tribe, and the tribe of Judah was taken; and he brought near the families of Judah, and the family of the Zerahites was taken; and he brought near the family of the Zerahites man by man, and Achan the son of Carmi, son of Zabdi, son of Zerah, of the tribe of Judah, was taken.' Here we have a precise indication of the names of all the representative groups with which each individual was involved and through which he existed. By narrowing down the groups one by one it is possible to discover who must be expelled and eliminated so that Israel may become itself again, a political community of brothers engaged in that service of God which brings them liberation.

First, we are introduced to the tribe of Judah, one of the original twelve tribes which received the promised land of Canaan as an undivided heritage. The confederation of the twelve tribes has a twofold mission. It confesses belief in Yahweh, since it was Yahweh's intervention that changed a mass of wandering tribes into a people who were united neither by racial purity nor by the magnitude of their victories, but by loyalty to their faith. Israel is just one more of the peoples of the earth: 'A wandering Aramaean was my father' (Deut. 26.5); 'Your origin and your birth are of the land of the

Canaanites; your father was an Amorite, and your mother
a Hittite' (Ezek. 16.3). Israel is not a great or powerful people:
'It was not because you were more in number than any other
people that the Lord set his love upon you and chose you, for
you were the fewest of all peoples' (Deut. 7.7). But Israel, the
federation of the twelve tribes, confesses God in accordance
with the truthfulness of his name: 'And beware lest you lift up
your eyes to heaven, and when you see the sun and the moon
and the stars, all the host of heaven, you be drawn away and
worship them and serve them, things which the Lord your God
has allotted to all the peoples under the whole heaven. But the
Lord has taken you, and brought you forth out of the iron
furnace, out of Egypt, to be a people of his own possession'
(Deut. 4.19f.). The twelve tribes together confess their alle-
giance to faith in Yahweh. Together they are summoned for the
holy war, which is neither a war of racial superiority nor a war
of nationalistic expansion, but a war waged in obedience to
God's promise. As such, it does not bring the pride of victory,
but demonstrates faithfulness to the word of the one who
summons his people, goes before them and gives them victory.
The tribe, then, is the first corporate grouping within Israel,
the people whose roots are a history which has been one of
conflict from its beginnings: the twelve brothers, sons of Jacob,
the last of the patriarchs.

After the tribes come the clans. In ancient times justice was
exercised at clan level. After the clans come the families,
perpetuated by the succession of children. Each individual
belongs to the house of his father and his ancestors. Finally,
each man appears by himself, the free agent whose actions
either confirm faith, justice and life, or disturb and destroy
them. The individual is not under constraint, since we see him
constantly maintaining or disrupting the solidarity of corporate
relationships. Everything that an individual does affects the
groups which include him, provide him with a place and really
do support him. Without the tribes it is impossible to confess
the faith; without the clans there can be no justice; and without
the families, life cannot be perpetuated.

Within the fratriarchy, there is a constant transition from 'I' to 'we'; it is as if the 'I' were personified in the 'we' who express it and bring it together. There is a marvellous expression of this in the well-known confession of faith in Deuteronomy, in which the text appears both as a corporate confession and an individual cry, while passing as a narrative description: 'A wandering Aramaean was my father; and he went down into Egypt and sojourned there, few in number; and there he became a nation, great, mighty and populous. And the Egyptians treated us harshly, and afflicted us, and laid upon us hard bondage. Then we cried to the Lord the God of our fathers. . . And the Lord brought us out of Egypt. . . He gave us this land, a land flowing with milk and honey. And behold, now I bring the first of the fruit of the ground, which thou, O Lord, hast given me' (Deut. 26.5–10). Here the 'we' recalls the fratriarchy who confess the faith and by whom the conquest has been achieved. The 'I' expresses personal involvement in the recognition of this faith and in acknowledgment of this gift. Thus each Israelite finds his identity by belonging to the 'we', with its confession of the faith, its warlike character, its sense of the law and its vitality. However, this 'we' continues to live on the basis of the existence of the 'I'. It does not amount to an archaic or mythological explanation; it is a corporate form of human existence which is freely renewed in the context of the covenant. To belong to the group which refers to itself as 'we' brings blessings and integration, but the group is perpetuated only if the 'I's consent to it. All down history the fratriarchy imposes its restraints, but that does not mean that its evidential value is equally strong. What we have is a historical struggle, a constant threat from all those who do not regard themselves as their 'brothers' keepers' (Gen. 4.9), to echo the remark made by Cain in his indifference to Abel's murder. The fratriarchy observes the liberty of faith and not the voice of blood.

We can find confirmation of the importance of corporate groupings when we consider the fate of the isolated individual. The individual is essentially the one who suddenly discovers the threat of his solitude. Hardly has Cain renounced his

fraternal relationship with Abel, by killing him, than he
shrinks from the gulf which henceforth will separate him from
other people and make him the helpless victim of their vengeance. 'My punishment is greater than I can bear. Behold,
thou hast driven me this day away from the ground; and from
thy face I shall be hidden; and I shall be a fugitive and a
wanderer on the earth, and whoever finds me will slay me'
(Gen. 4.13f.). To be an isolated individual is to feel oneself
under threat: a fugitive, abandoned, an exile, separated,
hunted, at the gates of death and hell. Here are several typical
passages in which the Hebrew root *lebad*, 'solitary', constantly
recurs. Ahimelech the priest guesses that David is pursued by
Saul's jealousy: 'Why are you alone, and no one with you?'
(I Sam. 21.1). Similarly, Ahithophel, David's adviser, having
gone over to the camp of his rebellious son Absalom, rashly
promises the latter that he will kill David: 'I will come upon
him while he is weary and discouraged, and throw him into
a panic; and all the people who are with him will flee. I will
strike down the king only' (II Sam. 17.2). The psalmist
expresses his distress in a similar way: 'I am like a vulture of the
wilderness, like an owl of the waste places; I lie awake, I am
like a lonely bird on the housetop' (Ps. 102.7f.). This is also the
terrible condition of the leper, in so far as he has not been
reintegrated into the community of the living: 'He shall wear
torn clothes and let the hair of his head hang loose, and he
shall cover his upper lip and cry, "Unclean, unclean". He shall
remain unclean as long as he has the disease; he is unclean; he
shall dwell alone in a habitation outside the camp' (Lev.
13.45f.).

Solitude is abnormal and close to disaster. No one must ever
go forward alone; he must always be a member of society: of the
family, for the sake of his life and health; of the clan, for the
sake of justice and possessions; of the twelve tribes, for the sake
of faith and heritage. The Old Testament knows nothing of
romanticism and the blessings of solitude far away from
crowds and institutions. Solitude is always a threat and a
curse, separating a man from the supports to his life, hiding him

from God and cutting him off from the people. Salvation is a cure for solitude, showing God's face once again to the individual and restoring human relationships.

However, within the Old Testament we can also discover a solitude which is neither an abandonment nor an exclusion. On the contrary, it is an election, the first-fruits of a multitude to come. Here, those who go forward alone represent all those who will follow through the breach which has now been established. On the whole, these advances are made with reference to God, and an individual is seen to initiate or recapitulate the destiny of countless brethren. This is the case with Abraham, the father of a people, when on his own he leaves his ancestral home in old age (Gen. 12.1); with Noah, when on his own he finds favour at the time of God's wrath and the flood (Gen. 6.8); with Moses, when on his own he climbs Sinai to hear the voice in the cloud (Exod. 19.20); and with Jesus, when on his own he prays in Gethsemane as he fights against the twofold temptation of flight and death (Matt. 26.36). To outward appearances, all these solitary figures have been abandoned, but in fact they represent particular communities. They may seem to be excluded and rejected, but in reality they are the faithful remnant of the ancient people of God and the germ of a new people. The texts use the same word as before, *lebad*, for Abraham, 'for when he was but one I called him and blessed him' (Isa. 51.2); for Jacob at the ford of Jabbok (Gen. 32.24); for Moses on Sinai (Ex. 24.2); for Jeroboam receiving ten pieces of the prophet Ahijah's garments as a prophecy of the formation around him of the northern kingdom with its ten tribes (I Kings 11.29ff.); for Jeremiah, caught up alone by the power of Yahweh (Jer. 15.17). In all these examples, solitude, which takes the form of a rejection, amounts to an announcement. The most famous example of all is the one who in man's eyes is the dregs of humanity, but in God's eyes its nucleus: 'We esteemed him stricken, smitten by God, and afflicted . . . by his knowledge shall the righteous one, my servant, make many to be accounted righteous' (Isa. 53.4,11). The solitary figure who seems to be rejected will bear

fruit in the future, so even this passage confirms that in the Old
Testament every man is a representative of the political group
comprised by his brothers. He is the first-born who is to come,
even if he seems to be rejected and excluded.

The task of faith is to maintain the original heritage undivided
through history. There are divisions everywhere; each tribe has
its territory, each clan its locality and each family its line. But
the group as a whole must remain within the confederation of
the alliance; it has to be renewed constantly as generations
come and go. The loss of a tribe is a catastrophe to be remedied
as quickly as the eleven apostles remedied their situation after
the ascension by choosing a twelfth to replace Judas (Acts
1.16–26). The loss of a descendant is a catastrophe to be overcome with every possible means. The Old Testament describes
the perseverance of those involved without ever being astonished
at their evident immorality. The loss of an ancestral property is
a catastrophe which the poor smallholder will not accept, even
in the face of the anger and greed of the queen and the king
(Naboth refuses to surrender 'the inheritance of his fathers' to
Jezebel and to Ahab (I Kings 21.4)). All these lines converge
on the same point: the preservation of the reality of what was
given as the shared inheritance of all the brethren. There can
be only one political theology: the need to safeguard the
essence of corporate life despite and along with all territorial,
historical, and personal differences. This is not a matter of the
patriarchal respect owed to those who are older or more
powerful; but it amounts to the need within the fratriarchy of a
life which is lived by one for all and all for one.

Conflicts between brothers and between generations

This is why the great political drama of the Old Testament is
not the progressive erosion of patriarchal structures, but
continual conflicts between brothers. If Greek tragedy acts out
and teaches the way in which generations transmit the hereditary crimes of parents to their children, biblical history teaches
how in each generation brother attacks brother, while parents

either suffer because they have no means of expressing their love in the situation or take sides with their favourite child and from that point exercise a personal preference. Here there is no timeless tragedy of a constantly repeated destiny, such as we find among the Greeks. Here we encounter the temporal dramas of a heritage which almost always leads to conflict. The political history of the Old and New Testaments is dominated by hostility between pairs of brothers, rather than by oppressive parents. So we have Cain and Abel; Lot and Abraham; Ishmael and Isaac; Esau and Jacob; the eleven brothers and Joseph; Saul, Jonathan and David; Amnon, Tamar and Absalom (II Sam. 13); Jerusalem, Samaria and Sodom (Ezek. 16); the eleven apostles and Judas; James, Peter and Paul. There is an interminable list of brothers and sisters who are suspicious, jealous, aggressive, murderous towards one another, and who henceforth find themselves separated from the common heritage which ought to bind them together. It seems that the life of the family is simply a long series of rivalries, eliminations and constant losses.

It is worth spending some time on discovering why such wars arise and how they develop, since they never follow the course of an inevitable destiny; they are always started up again by free men who show themselves incapable of overcoming their bitterness. They flare up when the fire of jealousy is kindled by hatred arising out of differences. This is the case with Cain and Abel in an incident which so disturbs us, though we understand it well enough. Cain the labourer cannot control his anger against Abel the shepherd, whose sacrifice God, without any obvious reason, prefers (Gen. 4.4). However, God also speaks directly to Cain when he asks him why he is so downcast.

Thus the root of the first fratricide in the Bible will be an inability to cope with jealous fantasies provoked by the existence of real differences. Cain is the central figure in the story because it is from his stormy heart that pacification or fury will arise. Abel and the acceptance of his sacrifice are merely the occasion for Cain's choice. If there is sin and not destiny here, it is because Cain's capacity for free action is aroused by the

question which God puts to him. It is not because Cain has to
pay for the incomprehensible and despotic whims of a God
who has preferred Abel's sacrifice. God is not the source of
Cain's 'fall'. It is the difference in their situations which
engenders jealousy between the brothers. Jealousy would not
grow if there were not this initial fratriarchy, this invitation to
live in brotherhood, and if the differences were not so near to
home. Jealousy is born of comparison at close quarters. Being
human is to be involved in conflict, because that is the way
brothers are. There is ample evidence of this in the way wars
are waged: they are much more savage when they are civil
wars fought on territorial, religious or ideological issues.

The Bible suggests a second reason for the break-up of the
fratriarchy: competition over something that is in short supply.
In these stories about hostile brothers, there is competition for
the divine blessing. It cannot be extended to all the brothers,
and therefore becomes the prize over which they quarrel and
around which they manoeuvre. If everyone cannot share in the
inheritance, the last have to supplant the first and snatch by
stratagem and sacrifice what they cannot enjoy by right and by
nature. Here too, the arbitrariness of God's arrangements seems
at first sight to be the source and the cause of division and
unhappiness among men. The scarceness of the divine blessing
in theology is an exact parallel to the scarceness of earthly goods
available in an economy that God seems to have made as one
more factor which contributes to the break-up of humanity. In
the earlier instance, the divine whim seemed to provoke
psychological jealousy. Here divine parsimony seems an
incitement to materialistic competition. However, in the Bible
it is always wrong to see the indeterminate interplay of free
individuals as the workings of an inevitable destiny. The first-
born is not destined to lose, even though he may be called
Ishmael, Esau, or Saul; nor is the last-born destined to win,
even though he may be called Isaac, Jacob or David. We have
to recognize that the human fratriarchy always exists against a
background of scarcity, and that even the so-called affluent
society is the setting for a potential struggle between those who

risk losing their advantages and those who try to take these advantages from them. The Bible is not the story of a dynastic succession within which the heirs hand down their initial advantages from generation to generation; it describes a series of competitive situations in which the late-comers often get the better of those who are first in line with the fragility of their legitimate claim. It seems that nothing can dispel the anxiety of those who are to be deprived, even if the late-comers make every effort to keep the peace. We can see this from David's behaviour towards Saul. Thus the fratriarchy is torn apart, not only by jealous differences, but also by the scarcity of precious commodities.

We can find a thousand causes for human conflict. We might emphasize the fear of losing territory and a position of dominance; the struggle to dispossess those who enjoy some scarce commodity; or the monopoly situation of the upper classes and the exploitation of the workers. This would depend on whether we are more impressed by the arguments of animal biology; the existentialism of Sartre; or the Manichaeism of Marx. At this point I need not pass judgment on the validity of the various explanations; I am simply underlining the way in which brothers seem to seize every opportunity of destroying their brotherhood. A history of conflict develops out of an undivided inheritance. Human politics consists first in coming to terms with the fact that the brotherhood itself nourishes war. The wisdom literature confirms the story of the prophetic books: 'All a poor man's brothers hate him; how much more do his friends go far from him! He addresses supplications to them, but they disappear' (Prov. 19.7).[10] 'Better is a neighbour who is near than a brother who is far away' (Prov. 27.10). Hatred among brothers is a tenacious reality. Without doubt it is nearer to the root of conflict than the struggle between master and slave. That seems to be more of a detached affair, in which the disrupted fraternity takes refuge behind what it puts forward as a hierarchical statute. That is then succeeded by another unacknowledged hierarchy or a hypocritical claim to total equality. In this situation, the master is not the only

one to be blamed, nor is the slave truly innocent. The problem
goes back to the brother who is the object of hatred provoked
by a thousand very real instances of differences and jealousy,
scarcity and competition. This root of hatred between brothers
is a threat to God's holiness among his political people: 'You
shall not hate your brother in your heart. . . You shall not take
vengeance or bear any grudge against the sons of your own
people, but you shall love your neighbour as yourself: I am
the Lord' (Lev. 19.17f.).

Finally, we should add that this situation of conflict can also
be found between the generations, which confirms that the Old
Testament is not so much impregnated with respect for
patriarchal authority as permeated with reactions which
alienate those who are closest to one another. It is a book of
disorder, not of patriarchal order. The fathers are far from
being wise, respectable and perfect. Their sins fall on their
children. 'What wrong did your fathers find in me that they
went far from me, and went after worthlessness, and became
worthless?' (Jer. 2.5 – also 3.25; 11.10). Everything is turned
upside down. The blessing is not handed on from generation to
generation. On the contrary, the curse descends from the oldest
to the youngest. Hosea recommends the children to take legal
action against their adulterous mother (2.2), and Ezekiel warns
them against the practices of their parents: 'And I said to their
children in the wilderness, Do not walk in the statutes of your
fathers, nor observe their ordinances, nor defile yourselves with
their idols' (20.18). The generations to come will pay the price
for those which have gone before (Exod. 20.5; 34.6; Deut.
5.9): 'Our fathers sinned, and are no more; and we bear their
iniquities' (Lam. 5.7). 'The fathers have eaten sour grapes, and
the children's teeth are set on edge' (Ezek. 18.2; Jer. 31.29).
In these circumstances the patriarchy becomes a calamity,
since belonging to it is imprisonment and the inheritance a
bondage. Corporate guilt is as real in its consequences as it is
unjust at its foundations. There is a long strand of failure and
faithlessness which from now on chokes and corrupts. Whereas
the history of Israel begins, at the exodus from Egypt, as a

happy remembrance of the miracles done by God for the parents to the advantage of their children, it ends, at the deportation to Babylon, as an unhappy remembrance of offences committed against God by parents to the detriment of their children. Support has become a burden, and the outcome is a dead end. The sin of the fathers is certainly not disguised in these stories, which are so wrongly held to be steeped in patriarchal authoritarianism.

The fact that the fathers have fallen does not mean that their children will be any better. The mistakes of the former are no guarantee of the success of the latter. The corruption of old age does not create the innocence of youth. There is no more youthful pride than patriarchal respect in these stories in which God unmasks the reality behind the appearances. The parents may inflict the consequences of their sins on the children, but the children fail to live up to their parents' expectations. 'How can I pardon you? Your children have forsaken me, and have sworn by those who are no gods' (Jer. 5.7). 'But the children rebelled against me; they did not walk in my statutes, and were not careful to observe my ordinances, by whose observance man shall live' (Ezek. 20.21). In Deuteronomy, immediately after the very traditional ordinance that the child of a man by a woman whom he does not love is to be recognized as the first-born if he is born before the son of the woman whom he does love, we find the astonishing description of the way in which the elders of the city are to put to death the rebellious child who does not listen to his father or mother (21.18–21). This terrible tendency to inflict execution which appears in the institutions and customs of the Old Testament therefore suggests that the children might not agree at all with either the authority of their parents or the wisdom of the ancients. This is death to the hope that one day future descendants might see the coming on earth of what the fathers and the men of old had only greeted afar off. David, king by grace, experienced the rebellion of Absalom and could not rediscover the way he longed to go, because Absalom was killed, against his orders and contrary to his desires: 'And as he went, he said, "O my son Absalom, my son, my son Absalom! Would I had died instead of you, O Absalom, my son, my son!"' (II Sam. 18.33).[11]

The faults of the fathers and the revolt of the sons finally leads to the corporate discouragement to be found among those, including the greatest, who express the despair of the generations which follow and resemble them: 'Did I conceive all this people? Did I bring them forth, that thou shouldst say to me, "Carry them in your bosom, as a nurse carries the sucking child, to the land which thou didst swear to give their fathers?"' (Num. 11.12). Elijah longs for death: 'It is enough; now, O Lord, take away my life; for I am no better than my fathers' (I Kings 19.4). Parents and children combine in acknowledging their joint failure. Each generation experiences afresh the disruption of the fratriarchy, the infidelity of the patriarchy and the deception of renewal.

Three models of reunion

However, the political model that we find here in the Old Testament does not give the impression of being one of successive decadence, of the type that we find, for example, in accounts by Greek philosophers of the progressive degeneration of cities from their original ideal constitutions. Still less does it appear as a tragic necessity, presented as a series of useless heroic interludes against a background of inexorable destiny. The political model of the broken fratriarchy has quite a different connotation from social decadence or tragic necessity. To keep within the specific dimensions of human history, which we sometimes forget when we talk too readily of the reconciliation accomplished by God, it might be best to describe it as a model of reunions between hostile brothers. Reunions between brothers are the human course by which situations are transformed in a revolutionary and creative way.

The Bible describes reunions between brothers as well as political collapse within the fratriarchy. There is a restoration of the lost link, without which one domination can only lead to another, to elimination and oblivion. These reunions imply rupture and loss, but they exclude suppression and substitution. They make up the political model of a revolution which does not seek to dominate the adversary but to rediscover him; which does not seek to judge the enemy, but to restore relations with him. And the way to this is not through magnanimity, nor through brain-washing, but through a profound awareness of being part of the undivided inheritance of the fratriarchy, which has been broken and then restored.

The Old Testament, then, describes how brothers are reunited. Its messianism does not look to a sublimation of the human condition, but to a restoration of brotherhood in liberty and equality. The revolution does not issue in the disappearance of some and the idealization of others, but a great reunion. For the prophetic and apocalyptic books, the gathering together of those who have been scattered is one of the major signs of the last time. The final verse of the Old Testament deals with these reunions, 'Behold, I will send you Elijah the prophet before the great and terrible day of the Lord comes. And he will turn the hearts of fathers to their children and the hearts of children to their fathers, lest I come and smite the land with a curse' (Mal. 4.5f.).

But how do these reunions between hostile brothers in the Old Testament come about? Let me use three different examples to illustrate the model. First, there is the model of the protection of the guilty party and of patience with the destroyer. This happens in the case of Cain. We have seen how he finds the prospect of solitude terrifying and menacing. So God puts on him a token of legal protection: 'Then the Lord said to him, "Not so! If anyone slays Cain, vengeance shall be taken on him sevenfold"' (Gen. 4.15). Justice begins when vengeance is choked off. However, the fratricide, guilty and alone, is not exterminated, since at the appointed time Cain's descendants will be reunited with Abel. And according to the biblical theme, we are all the descendants of Cain, destined for reunion with the descendants of Seth, Abel's substitute (Gen. 4.25). So the elimination of one brother is not followed by the elimination of the other. Rather, as one might put it, the guilty party is given protection, is left in suspense, and a substitute is found for the innocent victim, so that the fratriarchy can at least remain the horizon against which each life can be lived out. The judicial model of patience, protection even within punishment, seeks to impose sanctions without bringing about destruction, to quench the vindictive anger of the vendetta in order to move towards the ultimate dream of descendants who will live together. However, this first model remains an extremely meagre one. It is opposed to the extermination of the guilty party, but it does not open up any way towards a reunion. It protects the guilty party; it saves him from lynching but does not reintegrate him into the common life.

Now comes the second model, which I shall call that of the prudent approach. The case study here is that of Jacob, meeting after fourteen years his elder brother Esau, whom he has deceived, robbed and humiliated. Jacob knows that human reconciliation is not primarily a matter of one party extending pardon; this could still be seen as an act of condescension. The important thing is to accept pardon, to put oneself – as in so many instances – in the position of one who is also in the wrong. First Jacob struggles with the angel of God, so that the power of the divine reconciliation which he thus receives will allow him to attempt reunion. Bearing his new name, Israel, the one who struggles with God (Gen. 32.38), Jacob seeks reconciliation with Esau. The attempt takes place in three stages. Jacob diplomatically brings a large number of presents, to smoothe the way with Esau. The great emotional reconciliation then takes place, and Esau is the first to run, fall on his brother's neck and embrace him. However, there is yet a third element in this prudent approach. Jacob does not forget that the remembrance of grievances can overshadow the emotional effect of a reunion. So he declines Esau's suggestion that they should continue their journey together and proposes that although they have re-established relations, the brothers should continue to keep their distance. The victory achieved over God (in a word, the blessing) does not remove the difficulty of ongoing coexistence with a hostile brother (in a word, history). The second model goes some way beyond the first, since not only has the guilty party (in fact there are two guilty parties) been saved, but a reunion has been achieved. However, the restoration of the fratriarchy remains such a fragile business that from now onwards each brother settles a long way from the other.

The third model is the best illustration of the way in which the revolution of reunion in fact transforms murder into salvation and death into life. The case study here is Joseph being reunited with the brothers who have sold him in order to get rid of him. Joseph has since become the Pharaoh's steward, and now has his brothers at his mercy. The brothers are afraid that Joseph will exploit his position of power over them in the same way as they once exploited theirs over him. But Joseph turns the situation upside down and revolutionizes it. In order to restore the fratriarchy he turns a possible opportunity for vengeance into a chance of real salvation: 'And he said, "I am your brother, Joseph, whom you sold into Egypt. And now do not be distressed, or angry with yourselves, because you sold me here; for God sent me before you to preserve life"' (Gen. 45.5). Here the broken fraternity, simply by being broken, becomes the foundation of a reunited fratri-archy. We have gone beyond patience and prudence. We see the reunion re-establishing a communication which had seemed to be cut off, a communion which had seemed to be lost. The lively fratriarchy involving the twelve sons of Jacob forms the basis for the confessing and fighting confederacy of the twelve tribes of Israel. Similarly, the fratriarchy comprising the twelve apostles and Jesus of Nazareth, which is also rent by treason and treachery, until it is restored by the transformation of the cross into salvation and resurrection, forms the basis for the confessing and fighting community of the church.

In this third model we find a total reintegration of the guilty parties so that they become agents and witnesses of a revolution which does not aim to eliminate or to subjugate one side or to install and favour the other, but to re-establish and consolidate those who had been scattered and crushed. If we understand revolution in a radical sense, not so much (or not only) as a change in a particular mode of production, but rather as a change, an upheaval in a mode of coexistence, we shall find that the experiences of the fratriarchy according to the Bible, and especially in the Old Testament, are the model *par excellence* for political revolution. Here man is upheld by patience, prudent in renewing contact, and overcome when reunion is achieved. Certainly, this is a difficult political model and a costly revolution. It is easier to use the law to get people out of the way, constantly to suspect and abuse, than to protect the guilty, negotiate with neighbours and make peace with enemies. One can hardly say, however, that this is an idealistic model, in the sense that it retreats into a sphere of values which have no power to transform situations. Here we have a realistic history, because it is the only one capable of making a radical transformation. In making the reconstruction of the fratriarchy the revolutionary goal of human politics, ignoring neither its constant disruptions nor its constant renewal, the Old Testament contributes to political theology a history of conflicts in which the cohumanity of all the brethren is broken and remade.

Holding on under pressure

My remarks about the New Testament must be more brief. Its objective is to teach men not so much how to achieve transformations by revolution as to show patience, vigilance and endurance in a situation where they are under constant pressure. It is not difficult to explain this change of perspective, though it might at first sight seem amazing, indeed deceitful and scandalous, that after the advent of 'messianic times' with the Jesus of the gospels we find the first Christians continuing to live within the restraints of their age. A partial explanation of this is that one section of the primitive church was convinced that the period of history before the return of Christ would be brief, and that as a result, it was not worth planning anything. Waiting was the only answer. At the same time, however, it was important for the mission of the church that those who were converted to Christ should have an answer to their non-Christian neighbours. The latter suspected that people were converted in the expectation of some personal benefit: that by joining a new brotherhood they hoped to escape the pressures of an ongoing society which sanctioned slavery, the patriarchal authority of the husband over the wife, the payment of tax to the imperial government, and all the other arrangements by which ancient society regulated relationships to suit itself. So the first Christians felt obliged to live in the Lord under these constraints, instead of withdrawing from them in favour of their new faith. Beyond question, believers were also loyal and positive towards a series of regulations and authorities. They asked for their faith to be respected and tried to avoid idolatry, but they did not expect the authorities to disappear or to be replaced. Finally, and above all, they were realistic about the political situation. The young Christian community was a barely tolerated minority which was progressively persecuted. In such a situation, political realism was not so much a matter of dreaming of revolution as of living with persecution; in other words, not giving way to the escapism of a religious dream but accepting the realities of political history. That is why the problem of political pressures seems to me to be as central to the New Testament as the problem of fratriarchal revolution is to the Old.

Let me take as an example a book which seems to run completely counter to my proposition: the book of Revelation, the Apocalypse. We know that for Engels,[12] Revelation was the most revolutionary book of the New Testament, concealing behind a religious vocabulary the radical protest of the oppressed masses against the imperialist power of Rome. At first sight, then, it might seem absurd to look to the book of Revelation for a political theology concerned with the continuance of the present constraints. However, this is the direction taken by Ernst Käsemann, whose suggestions I follow here.[13] He reconstructs the probable development of theological reflection within the growing church in the following way. First of all, during his lifetime, Jesus will have differed from John the Baptist in placing less emphasis on the imminence of the kingdom. Rather than issuing a summons to repentance, Jesus stressed the signs of grace in the present, which brought a welcome and liberation of sinners. By contrast, after Christ's resurrection, the first Christians will have been thrown into a state of post-Easter enthusiasm, greeting the birth of the new people of the last times. Käsemann believes that, as a third stage, the mission among Jews and Gentiles will have soon involved Christians in two difficult debates: in Jewish circles on the significance of the law, and in Gentile circles on the fruits of the spirit. Hence the fourth stage (for Käsemann, the anthropological developments of Paulinism and the historical and cosmological developments of Revelation), which will have been dominated by a preoccupation with survival under permanent constraints. Revelation, in particular, will have been written above all to encourage a realistic view of the present. It postpones the date of the final dénouement, a delay which is indicated by the repetition of series of sevens;[14] these qualify premature enthusiasm in the present time by saying 'not yet' and pointing to the future. That is why, if Käsemann's reconstruction (or fabrication) is correct, the book of Revelation lays so much stress on perseverance, which is neither surrender nor impatience. It would strengthen a political capacity to hold on while the constraints were still in force; they were not expected to go on for ever, but for the moment they were tempting and burdensome. In that case, Revelation would not be a febrile expression of millenarian mysticism, but a temperate exhortation to perseverance in Christian belief despite the pressures which continued and were constantly renewed. In that case it would provide *the* political model for resistance when revolution was impossible and even unthinkable.

I cannot prove that Käsemann is right in seeing a connection between the Pauline epistles and Revelation, which are so often contrasted. In the eyes of Marxist historians, at any rate, Revelation is a revolutionary work, at one extreme of the New Testament writings, whereas the Pauline epistles, with their conservative and even Constantinian approach, lie at the other. Here again, Käsemann's hypothesis has the advantage of establishing at a deep level a connection between two streams which otherwise seem to diverge completely and apparently suggest two completely different models for the history of the church to follow. Otherwise, St Paul would seem to have inaugurated a conservative Christianity and Revelation would seem to have promised a revolutionary one. I have been particularly concerned to keep to the political theme of constraint. The important thing here is that by virtue of its christological insights, political theology should continue to acknowledge the presence of constraint without hallowing it out of necessity, or pretending that it is a dream. It was the crucified Jesus who supported the opposition in a confession which showed no signs of weakness. His perseverance alone was neither a Stoic indifference to external situations nor a Zealot enthusiasm which took its rejection of political constraint to the point of heroic despair. Nor was it a demonstration of non-violence, since Jesus suffered violence without expecting to break it by non-resistance. Here political theology finds a model to strive for which shows how it is possible to live under constraint without either denying it or breaking it. For the way of the cross is also a political course, since it recognizes the narrow limits imposed by constraints, and the loss which these can cause in life and death. Nevertheless, Christians persevere along this narrow route, assailed by persecutions, incapable of revolution and yet saved from resignation. So in the New Testament, the letters of Peter and Paul and the postponements announced in Revelation have one thing in common: the climate of constraint experienced in the company of Jesus Christ, which may even lead to the cross.

I have retained two very different political models: the revolutionary reunions of the fratriarchy, according to the Old Testament; and perseverance in Christ despite all pressures, according to the New Testament. At first sight, these two models are in conflict, since the reunions transform situations, whereas perseverance defers hope. However, both models seem necessary elements of any political theology which seeks a foundation in truth rather than a legitimation on grounds of necessity, which seeks to renew the world as well as to hang on despite its destruction; which seeks to act as well as to support; which seeks revolution as well as persistency, in accordance with Mao Tse Tung's famous dictum: 'Revolution requires a good deal of patience.' So it is false to contrast revolutionary optimism with conservative pessimism. The next thing is to practise both resistance and submission, depending on the circumstances, what they require and what they make possible.

3

Relating the Bible to Contemporary Situations

Development takes place when there is tension, when life is not a matter of continuation or imitation, but of transition. We must now go on to consider the transition from the message of the texts to the existence they transform, using appropriate methods for mapping out this transition. In the previous chapter we anticipated, by examining the content of the biblical texts first. However, it is no bad thing to talk about method after covering some of the ground. One runs two risks in preambles about methodology. First, methods might be supposed to guarantee a safe crossing, whereas they never do more than suggest a possible itinerary. Secondly, and above all, the methodology is concerned to check how a journey may be made: formal cartography with its clear lines is no substitute for the discovery of unknown continents. Reading is an interesting occupation, not only in order to make up structuralist grid-patterns and compare them, but also in order to listen to what is actually said.

Metaphysical and historical tension

There are various kinds of tension. The most classical of them is metaphysical by nature. This is the contemplative tension between the mixed world of the senses in which man lives, and the pure world of the intelligence to which he aspires. Platonism remains the most famous example. It influenced Western culture with its contrast between matter and idea, accident and essence, the One (or the synoptic) and the many.[15] It also influenced Christian theology, which used these very categories to illustrate the difference between the creature and the Creator, between man and God. According to this classical tension, we are material beings, contingent and corruptible; our souls aspire to rediscover their original and forgotten country while living in the body and being bound up with it. Only the contemplative way can illuminate life, direct its course and guide immortal souls on their journey to the eternal harbour. I shall not say much here about this first contemplative voyage. Culturally we no longer live in the period of classical metaphysics and its predominant influence on Christian theology, along with the risks it knew so well: to take up the two poles of the Platonic journey, there were the dangers of confusing sin with a descent into the world of matter, and similarly, of assimilating life in faith to the ascent towards a vision of the world of ideas.

In modern times we usually find another tension. We might best describe it as being meta-historical, or rather meta-prehistorical, always referring to what can be found in the future which lies beyond. According to this second perspective, humanity and the universe are still at a stage of prehistory. In due course we shall see the beginning of the true history of liberated humanity. The important thing is to transform the present structures of society, which in subjective terms are alienated and in objective terms are exploited, to usher in this true society of the future, which is scientifically possible. In revolutionary terms, however, it is fragile, since the prospect of it disappears once man gives up fighting against the oppressive structures which hold him back. Its coming is seen in terms of the end of the unjust division between social classes (as opposed to the impure mixture of the senses and the intellect which we find in metaphysics, just as the struggle to transform history takes the place of the contemplative asceticism of the soul). This Marxist vocabulary is as common in modern times as was Platonic terminology in the classical period. The tension is no longer between the transitoriness of temporal existence and the rediscovery of eternity, but between present prehistory, with its contradictions and injustices, and future history, when there will be an end to alienation. Future history will certainly continue to include struggles, but from then on they will be carried on by a united community, with no division between classes, against a nature which needs to be humanized, so that man himself can once again become natural, enjoying the fruits of his labour and the many aspects of culture.

One classic form of Christianity used the categories of the contemplative ascent to express, with variable success, the conversion of man to God. Similarly, one form of contemporary Christianity uses the categories of the transformation of history, again with variable success, to express the progress of the church and the world towards the kingdom. I say 'with variable success' in each case, since the good news which comes from God tends to crumble as soon as it is assimilated too readily to the culture in which it is communicated. Contemplative culture runs the risk of disincarnating God (and man in turn) by associating the world of the senses too closely with earthly desires, just as it runs the risk of spiritualizing God (and, in a parallel way, man) by associating the world of the intellect with the heavenly vision. In our time, 'revolutionary' culture runs the risk of making the hope of faith abstract by associating it too closely either with the 'scientific' laws of history or the 'utopian' expectation of an idealized future. Certainly we need to express the tension which the reality of God imposes on man in the language of the culture of our time. But we should not suppose that this culturally-conditioned language, with the relative tensions which are part of its make-up (at one time that between the senses and the intellect, and now that between the present and the future), can be an adequate vehicle for the encounter of God with man in his Word and of man with God in his act of hearing. Otherwise we would no longer be talking about God in a given culture; we would be making culture the mouthpiece of God.

Living alongside the texts

I propose now to examine a third tension which is of a different kind. To make the parallel with the others clearer, I shall call it meta-textual tension. This is the interpretative tension experienced by men when they have to relate particular texts, with firm roots in the past, to a life which cannot be detached from its present. It is not a question here, as in metaphysics, of finding a way upwards from below, towards that primal situation of which we have some obscure memory and for which we have a great unsatisfied longing. Nor is it a question, as in meta-prehistory, of moving from the fragmentary present to a future consummation.[16] Meta-textual tension does not relate to another world overlapping into this one or to a future brought to birth through the present. It sets texts alongside life, applying their precise details to a vague generality and sowing their seed in our ground.

At first sight this development would seem to be less attractive and less imposing than the two previous examples. It does not involve an ascent towards the heavenly vision, nor does it envisage a tangible transformation; it seeks, rather, to sow seeds in the present. In reality, however, the distance here is greater. In this enterprise we can derive no comfort from the mystical or historic assurance that man is truly capable of attaining complete purity within himself or achieving revolution in the society around him. We do not know how the seed can germinate or how the ground can be fertilized: how the stem (the ancient text) can be grafted on to the tree (the present time). Will there be fruitful and creative tension? Will the texts end up robbing life of its content because they constrict it, or will life rob the texts of their content by assimilating them to such a degree that they are neutralized and forgotten?

When I use the phrase meta-textual tension, the 'meta' takes on a different meaning. It does not indicate a transcendence rising beyond obscurity and earlier alienation, as in metaphysical contemplation or in revolutionary transformation: 'meta' here means 'with', not 'beyond'. The texts are with us all our lives. To move on would be to forget, and to forget would involve the risk of changing our journey into an emigration bound for some intellectual heaven of ideas or a future stage of history. Meta-textual tension does not look for an emigration elsewhere, to heaven or to the future. It tries to listen here and now, on earth, in the present. Such an approach sees texts which are always with us as the material and 'canonical'[17] indication that God goes alongside man to help him understand the time in which he lives, and that man is brought up against a God who cannot be by-passed, but seeks to be known and believed in, to be followed and worshipped.

Committed listening

Before we go on to other aspects of the interpretative distance between ancient texts and present-day life, it is important to understand the chief reason for this distance, of which the texts are merely a specific indication. This distance would not in fact exist, and there would only be remoteness, to be overcome by an attempt at relevance, did these texts not confront those who read them on the presupposition that they would meet with committed attention. I use these concepts of presupposition and commitment as the equivalents of revelation and faith; they still need to be qualified. In so doing I run the risk of anticipating a conclusion which, in the strict logic of discovery and verification, I should only arrive at later. Surely, the so-called 'canonical' texts should be read in the same way as any other texts, leaving aside all biased presuppositions, since anyone who has beliefs of his own when reading them risks attributing to them a significance which in fact arises from his decision to regard them as sacred writings. This is a legitimate objection, but there seems to me to be an even more legitimate counter-attack. It acknowledges that those who study such texts approach them with some degree of commitment and on the presupposition that the text will have something particularly significant to say.

The readers of the Bible (or of the Koran, if they are Muslims)

do not find in the text a sacred character which they project on
to it. They do, however, recognize that their approach is a
committed one. They have no guarantee that these texts will
communicate a divine revelation to their human faith, but
they affirm that they approach them with a stronger commitment than a mere curiosity for knowledge. This opens up the
way for a promising communication. That is why I have felt it
legitimate to compare meta-textual tension with metaphysical
and meta-historical tension. Here, too, there is the prospect of a
metamorphosis. However, it is not concentrated either on a
heavenly vision or on a transformation of the future. Granted,
at a given time contemplation and revolution can be an
adequate expression of the effect which the texts have on a
man. But I want above all to insist on the importance of living
with the texts today, with their external ruggedness and their
hidden fruitfulness. They recall to our lives the disconcerting
and life-giving outgoing of God himself.

The texts, then, lead to tension and development. For God is
not so much Being, the ultimate object of contemplation, or
Action, the transforming energy of history and nature, as a
sovereign Word, put forward in humility to be understood and
received. The tension of the presence of God is not experienced
'beyond', or 'ahead', but 'alongside': it is the presence of a
partner. 'For this commandment which I command you this
day is not too hard for you, neither is it far off. It is not in
heaven, that you should say, "Who will go up for us to heaven,
and bring it to us, that we may hear it and do it?" Neither is it
beyond the sea, that you should say, "Who will go over the sea
for us, and bring it to us, that we may hear it and do it?" But
the word is very near you; it is in your mouth and in your heart,
so that you can do it!' (Deut. 30.11–14).

It is in this precise sense that in the Bible God is called a
mystery, not in the modern sense of an enigma which is still
impenetrable in the beyond and still unaccomplished in the
future, but in the sense of an unveiling which is effected in the
midst of time. To quote St Paul: 'He has made known to us in
all wisdom and insight the mystery of his will, according to his

purpose which he set forth in Christ as a plan for the fullness of time, to unite all things in him, things in heaven and things on earth' (Eph. 1.9; cf. also I Cor. 2.1,7; 4.1; 13.2; Col. 1.26f.).

God's communication and man's responsibility

God seeks to communicate himself to man and achieves his purpose. This is what the Bible calls election and revelation, stripping these two words of their erroneous connotations of inexplicable arbitrariness and secret favour, and restoring their original positive sense. They point to decision and accomplishment in the context of a history whose texts both inform us and involve us. God 'guides' human history. His word is a rock against which the waves of the world break. By communicating himself through the medium of history, God relieves man of the need to think in other terms: of mythology here, of metaphysics in the beyond and of utopianism in the future. This communication makes human life a place for hearing. A distance is set up so that man may seek and be able to understand. Here communication is not essentially a contemplative reminiscence of something from beyond, nor is it a plan to transform what lies ahead; it is attention to the Word of another. However, this distance is also surmounted, because this Word does not just slip away: it takes the initiative. In these circumstances, man becomes the one who can respond by listening. By responding, he becomes responsible, since the etymology of responsibility is not rooted in a reclaiming of autonomy but in a readiness to hear and to respond. So we can see how human life which, while being detached from the texts and their otherness, is at the same time within hearing distance of them and in communication with them, becomes a responsible life which has the freedom and the calling to respond in the present to this God who manifests himself as Word.

What I have called meta-textual existence consists in a life lived in contact with texts which offer the possibility of communicating with a God who is a Word for us. We presuppose that God can show himself as Word through the biblical texts. Granted, God can and does speak in a thousand different ways, some of which are more coherent or seductive, more striking or more suited to our existence than the biblical texts. Anyone who denied that would deprive God of the freedom to take many forms. Only here, however, can we be sure of coming into contact over a distance with another who has resolved to make himself known. Two things are clear about the biblical texts: their unyielding character and their concern to communicate. That could be said just as well of a thousand other texts. But only the biblical texts focus, more or less clearly, on the communication of the mystery of God in that sector of human history which runs from the call of Abraham to the coming of Jesus Christ. They focus on the involvement in the world of a God who was made Word within that particular history.

We cannot move out of this circle, either to demonstrate that only this particular Word represents God in the midst of all the tumult of the world and history, or to fathom God to the point of being certain that his true nature is revealed in this Word and nowhere else. That would excuse us from taking the risk of believing it ourselves. At least, however, we can understand why what I have called meta-textual tension creates real otherness and knowledge with specific demands. It shows how the nature of God the Word is to communicate and how the man who listens to him has a real responsibility.

Metaphysical and meta-prehistorical distance do not seem to me to involve such consistent otherness or the same degree of communication. In such situations we either project our longing for eternity and our concern to change, or we experience only the pangs of a desire or the demands of a project. That is why the distance to be overcome by interpretation is a positive factor. It is not an obstacle or an embarrassment, and we do not have to hesitate about the best way of overcoming it. It is an opportunity, a favourable sign, an occasion for fruitful communication. What is involved here is not primarily spiritual asceticism or the transformation of history, but trying to listen to a God who is other than our aspirations or our energies, a God who transforms illusory autonomy into the acceptance of responsibility. This is the chief, beneficial reason for meta-textual existence, in which we are not led astray through by-passing the texts but are guided aright by resorting to them. Anyone who parts company from them risks putting his fancies in place of what he might hear; in other words, he substitutes his own hot-headedness for the patience of the God of Abraham, of Isaac, of Jacob and of Jesus Christ.

Historical and secular texts

Now we can go on to the other and, I think, more minor problems which trouble readers who seek to relate the biblical texts to present-day situations. First of all, these texts hardly seem like sacred writings (in the sense that sacred is the opposite of profane, immutable of changeable, primordial and archaic of circumstantial and historical). As we saw in the previous chapter, the biblical texts tell particular stories which never pass over into mythology or symbolism.[18] They describe unique episodes. They present their message in connection with given circumstances: the existence of a fratriarchal conflict among twelve tribes of Aramaean origin or the pressures on a community brought into being by a crucified man who was raised from death and oblivion. These are the specific circumstances, one might say the events, from which we must seek to discover a way towards a universalizable abstraction which might be called a political theology.

Furthermore, these events are reported to us in a variety of ways which do not always agree, by men who are limited to the specific task of witness and interpretation. A witness has the unique privilege of describing events as he experiences them, but this means that he is deprived of the opportunity to reflect on them at a philosophical level, just as he has to forgo those symbolic explanations which provide a feast for the imagination In fact the witness can only tell part of the story. The biblical witnesses, then, are led to speak and write under the pressure of the events which they experience. At the same time, however, they are also interpreters who write, not only to provide a record, but to testify to the meaning which they feel to be inherent in the events they witness and narrate. In their interpretation they re-enact, in the circumstances of their own time, the witness with which they are confronted, thereby adding proclamation to their testimony. For example, the four gospels are at the same time both a record of the oral tradition on which they are based and a proclamation directed to the various communities for which they were written.

To say that the biblical texts are secular is thus an indication that their nature is historical throughout. They do not disguise the particular circumstances in which they were composed. They therefore prove to be texts conditioned by an environment which might seem to limit their claims to universality. Their patent historical origin shows them to be witness, rather than speculation or fable. But it also presents us with the problem of moving from the texts, written at a particular time in a particular setting, to what they may mean for us today. Philosophical or symbolic texts do not present the same problem, because from the start they set out to be timeless and for all time.

This means, paradoxically, that the biblical texts set out to be sacred texts (because the chief reason for the distance to be bridged by interpretation is the presupposition that God makes himself known in them as Word), but do not look like sacred texts, since everything about them points to their historical situation, their rough-hewn testimony, and their localized interpretation. Their concern is sacred: to communicate to men the knowledge of a God who though apart from men yet speaks to them. Their genre is secular: they are occasional writings which make no attempt to disguise their historical origin or the way in which they are influenced by styles fashionable at the time when they were written.[19]

The first difficulty, then, is to relate such evident secularity to a sacred character which is equally manifest. This is the difficulty with any reading that one might call sacramental:

how does a specific action acquire a universal significance? How can a particular figure convey a decisive message without ceasing to be an event; without becoming a cypher, a symbol or a myth; without gaining in general significance what it will lose in its concrete, historical character? In short, how is it possible to speak to a universal audience without disregarding the uniqueness of what I have called canonical texts? This is the first methodological problem presented by the biblical texts.

Two testaments, two situations

The second problem concerns the difference between the New Testament and the Old. This is not a difference of content. In the course of the previous chapter we saw how the central message of the New Testament can be found in an incident in the Old, in this case a reunion between hostile brothers. We might go on to say that this history becomes more radical in the transition from the Old Testament to the New: whereas Joseph is simply sold, rejected and sent away by his eleven other brothers, Jesus is crucified, sacrificed and buried by the descendants of the sons of Abraham and Jacob, as representatives of the whole of humanity. That is why the surprising and disquieting reunion between Joseph and his brother is replaced in the New Testament by a resurrection which in human terms is impossible. Everything here becomes more radical: the loss, the reunion, the proclamation. But although it becomes more radical, the content is not changed. It is not as though we were passing from law to grace, from judgment to love. When something becomes more radical we see its roots, which have been there since the beginning of history, but now come clearly into view. Radicalization takes to extremes meanings which were previously hidden or unnoticed.

The content may not change, but the situation certainly does. The Old Testament is concerned with a particular people. The New Testament is addressed to all mankind. But here again, when talking of such a change, we need to be precise. We cannot say that the Old Testament is particularist and the New Testament universalist. In the Old Testament, every story sets out to be a mirror in which all the descendants of Adam (and not just those of Abraham, Isaac and Israel) can see themselves in God's light. Universalism is always latent in these stories which seem so particularist. Conversely, the New Testament is also the most particularist of histories, since it is concerned to express the universal significance of what begins with a unique outcast from Israel. It focusses on Jesus who was born in Bethlehem, brought up in Nazareth and executed in Jerusalem, and who never showed any desire to go further afield or to cover more ground for a longer period of time. We might say that the New Testament brings out even more the universalism contained in embryo form in the Old, but that it does so by never ignoring the roots of this universalism in a particularism to which it constantly refers. Jesus of Nazareth becomes the Christ announced to Israel and the Word which is the bread of the world. However, this Christ and this Word bear an individual name, Jesus.

The real difference between the two Testaments lies in the peoples involved in their texts. One is a people separated from others by its visible constitution. It has its own territory under its own control, even if the form of government often changed during its history: patriarchal confederation, charismatic judges, dynastic kings, rival kingdoms, exile, semi-independence and colonial occupation. The Old Testament contains texts addressed to a people with a theocratic government, in which religious and civil society combined to form a nation. The three great offices of king, priest and prophet were held on behalf of the whole of society, even if numerous currents, schools and ideologies divided the nation into opposing groups. The situation is different when we come to the New Testament texts. They are addressed to a people scattered among the nations of the world. The problem now is that of the relationship of a church which is not the state and which does not govern in its place, to a state which is not a church and which does not share its beliefs. Here, too, history will show numerous forms which this coexistence has taken: persecutions against Christians and loyalty on the part of the church towards civil society; then agreement and concordat, Christianity and a partial reconstruction of society on Old Testament lines with Christians concentrated in a particular geographical area; finally, the progressive secularization of the state and the missionary dissemination of the church, new persecutions and the threat that the churches will be forced to the periphery of life. All this has been realized through events, and shows how history makes a mock of schematic patterns. The problem posed by the New Testament as opposed to the Old inevitably remains the same: from now on there are two mixed societies instead of one gathered society.

Now we shall have to consider the difficulties which arise in the transition from Old Testament to New. How are we to know which Old Testament texts still have some significance, because in them God communicates a lasting Word, and which have become obsolete, because they were addressed by God to a theocratic nation which was subsequently replaced by a church dispersed among different civil societies? Calvin was fond of drawing a distinction here between the moral laws of the Old Testament, which were maintained and made more radical by the New; the civil laws, which were made obsolete because a new people grew up in place of those to whom the texts were addressed; and the ceremonial laws, which were also made obsolete by the coming of the Messiah. This last put an end to the Old Testament institutions of proclamation and promise: all those, for example, which are connected with the Temple and sacrifices, the land and inheritance, descendants and genealogies.

Then there are texts which have become obsolete because the people to whom they are addressed no longer occupy the same position in society, or because their original religious significance has been fulfilled. And there are texts which have abiding significance because God does not cease to communicate himself through them as Word. It is difficult to identify these precisely, as it is useful not to confuse obsolescence with uprootedness, or continuity with generalization. As we have said, the Old Testament has the same content as the New, but makes it more radical. The New Testament has the same concern as the Old to universalize something which is very precise and particular. Thus it would be against the intention of the texts to consign to oblivion anything that might appear too particular, and henceforward only to keep to generalizations with no roots in events which ask to be given a universal significance. We do, however, have to move from a theocratic society to a church dispersed among civil society without losing the roots of this Word which remain attached to unique events, and without replacing them by abstract norms. I said earlier that the New Testament makes the content of the Old more radical. At this point I should also point out that the Old Testament has within it the roots of the content of the New. Once again the twofold sense of the word 'root' appears: ultimate meaning and specific origin. We need to relate the texts to life in order for the plant to grow in its new ground without losing contact with the nature of its origins.

Secularization and marginalization

There is, finally, a third problem, of which we have become more aware today. This is the secularization which extends across global society. Like the earlier difficulty, it is one of situation rather than content: how is it possible to retain the universal dimensions of the Word of faith which make it a proclamation for the world rather than a marginal option, when present-day society banishes Christianity to the sidelines and reduces its past to folklore? In particular, is it possible to develop a political theology when other more potent forces, like the power of the decision-makers and the opposition of the working classes, or economy and ideology, determine politics to a much greater extent than theological language and the political models it suggests? It is even more important to avoid a situation in which theology merely provides a rubber stamp in accordance with the shifts of history. Having once fed the ancient virtues of prudence and patience to parties standing for law and order, it should not now administer the new ferments of insurrection and hope to those standing for change. This would be to make theology too political, by the addition of a mixture of remorse, opportunity and perhaps opportunism. That is no way of elaborating a political theology for a period of secularization.

Secularization can in fact take two forms. There can be a rationalistic and lay form, in which irrational and clerical influences are rejected; and there can also be a religious and ideological form, where factors other than faith and reason are evoked as social forces. There are many new secular religions, with their orthodoxies and their schisms, their legitimate hierarchies and their disputes, their creeds and their excommunications. Since there are these two very different kinds of secularization, it would be shirking the issue to talk only of the first form. In each case, however, theology seems to be marginal, whether it is regarded by rationalistic secularization as a survival of a supernatural animism, or whether it is labelled by irrational secularization as a system which is too dogmatic, too intellectual and too explanatory. These two forms of secularization put into sharp focus the fact that the Christian church lives in the perspective of the New Testament, where it has to take account of the forces which govern civil society without pining for the advent of some theocratic regime for the whole of society.

This is the positive significance of secularization. It makes it clear that the Word of God is disseminated in a field in which other seeds have been sown before it and beside it. In positive terms, this secularization is a sociological confirmation of the real theological status of the Word of God, a status which has become clearer since the New Testament. It is disseminated among the nations and earthly powers, no longer bound to a territorial group or ruling power. Secularization is a good illustration of the difficulty of passing from the Word of faith to a pluralist society, whether this society is conformist or sceptical. It involves moving, making the transition, from biblical particularity towards a plurality which may be either religious or atheistic. Secularization forces one to take account of this transition and obviously contributes towards it.

At the same time, it is also possible in the name of secularization to choose to deny biblical texts any social relevance. In that case, what the Christian community itself considers to be the Word of faith is regarded as a private opinion, responsible for the continuance of ecclesiastical imperialism because it is concerned with the whole of society and is directed towards it. In that case secularization tolerates the church only in a marginal context, where it is expected to restrict itself to the inner religious life of its members, abstaining from all outward-looking and 'worldly' expressions and actions. This kind of secularization sheds no light on the difficulties of moving towards a pluralist society. It simply forbids the move. It wants a church on the periphery of society, so that society can become and remain a closed society. The Christian community cannot accept this marginalization, which dissociates the Word from world history and which brings this history to an end with its own explanations or imaginings. Thus the movement of the Word towards a pluralist and secularized society must be maintained over against a suppression of the Word within an isolated ghetto and the constriction of society within unassailable conformism.

Perhaps the best way of taking account of these two aspects is to affirm the positive character of secularization and the harmfulness of secularism. We shall find things easier, and stop playing with words, if we remember that now as ever the content of the Bible has to be brought into contact with every social situation. For as we have seen in the previous chapter, the Bible offers models relevant to all nations.

The change of civilization

As a footnote to this discussion on the difficulties of meta-textual progress let me touch briefly on what seems to me to be the least troublesome problem: the difference between civilizations. It is usually accepted that the history of mankind comprises three great ages. First came the palaeolithic age, dominated by foraging and hunting, in which human lives were short and harassed by natural threats, with men and women perhaps being equally at risk. Perhaps there was even an element of matriarchy bound up with the magical mystery of life. Then came the neolithic age, with the development of culture and education, more extended and more stable economic and political institutions, and without question a patriarchy which reflected a masculine domination of law and economics. Finally, we have the industrial age, in which mass production invaded the world; institutions have become more democratic and expectations and frustrations are shared more equally between men and women. If this is the case, it is evident that, historically and culturally speaking, all the biblical texts belong to the second era. All the situations described in stories, laws and parables are neolithic situations, agricultural and pastoral.

We have to move, then, from these particular situations towards our present situation, which is also historically conditioned. We shall have to bear in mind the difference in methods of production, which are now more industrial; in the pattern of political life, which is more democratic; and in the relationship between men and women, which is more egalitarian. But I persist in thinking that the difficulty presented by this cultural transition is not as great as is often supposed. The important thing is to note how what I have called the neolithic age itself provides a variety of models, and above all how the Bible uses historically conditioned parables to embody a message the character of which is not in itself neolithic. It looks towards a new life which is not dominated by hate or by pursuit, which are such constant features of every era of humanity. I think that we have already seen sufficient evidence of this in connection with the restoration of political brotherhood in a human family rent by conflicts, or in connection with the acceptance by Christians of existing political and social constraints. There is certainly a transition to be made; the setting of the parable has changed. But the message which it contains remains the same. This message is neither palaeolithic primitivism nor neolithic patriarchalism, much less industrial productivity. It looks for the transformation of relationships among brothers, who are always caught up in hate and fear, always exposed to constraints, where hope fights against illusion and perseverance against resignation.

Work on the texts

Thus what I have called meta-textual existence is actually enriched by the encounter brought about through listening to texts with a message of their own and which convey a divine message on the presupposition of faith. The move from biblical texts to human situations is also made difficult by the historical character of the texts. Some go with the visible theocracy of the Old Testament and others with the missionary dissemination of the New. Finally, the secularization of society threatens theology with marginalization. There is always transition, tension, interpretation, the need to listen, to keep a distance so that the texts stand outside us, without our losing touch with them. The transition is achieved by theological work. Theologians study the texts without forgetting them or repeating them, by implanting them in new contexts. They invite all men to consider these texts not as sacred writings to be revered in a timeless way, but as holy scripture to be related to history.

Theology is an attempt to use the texts not in a contemplation of the beyond or in a transformation of the world postponed into the future, but as a catalyst for the present day. This concern certainly centres on a vision of the glory of God, but its context is that of a renewal of history. I have tried to remain close to the source of this vision and the root of this renewal, that is to say, to the texts, seeing them not as bandages which mummify life, but as stems grafted on to our life to produce a growth in knowledge, to affirm, strengthen and bring about the will of God for us, with us and in us. Relating the texts to life thus both raises difficulties and forges links. They are rough-hewn and at a distance from us, yet to listen to them brings enrichment. Meta-textual life, life in accord with the texts, is like walking a tightrope: we must keep a balance between the possibility that we may swallow God up in culture, and the possibility that God may annihilate man by containing him within texts.

Nature, future and analogy

To conclude, let me give three examples of the way in which this transition is made, in order to elaborate a political theology. First, one can look to the texts for light on the forgotten destiny of our nature. This is brought to the attention of believers by the law of God, and to the attention of non-believers by the voice of their conscience, as Paul puts it in his letter to the Romans, where he is speaking of Jews and Greeks. In appealing to this idea of nature, the texts expect a universal political outcome, since every man, whether he is a believer (Jew) or an unbeliever (Greek), will find himself in the same position. In a situation where Christians were on the periphery of society or in a minority, one might go on to develop a general political theology based on the common good which took its bearings from the specific character of human nature. It might be possible to develop a natural law expressing the political values which were to be maintained and promoted. If person and community are inscribed in the nature of one and all, this law might seek to prevent the negative collectivism of individuals and the negative individualism of communities. The advantages of such a political theology are evident: it goes beyond the circle of believers and gives clear directions to a pluralist society made up of non-believers, for which the biblical texts provide a profound scriptural confirmation of man's nature, which is held to have been misunderstood or obscured. Thus political theology will essentially be a reminder of the natural norms of human existence, illustrated from appropriate biblical passages.

However, there are two obstacles to such an approach. The first is specifically biblical. Even in St Paul, the appeal to conscience and nature (much less the appeal to the law) does not add up to a positive position which is recognized and acknowledged. This appeal points to an impossible situation, a condemnation which is a prelude to the salvation of sinners by the grace of God alone. We may therefore ask whether the argument from human nature is as illuminating or as effective as is supposed. Does not the contrast between what is natural and what is contrary to nature conceal a much more real and much more decisive contrast: that between grace and sin? Does a political theology based on natural law go as far towards the roots of the matter as the expression and action of the Word of God? It runs the risk of reducing the history of salvation to a reminder of the good advice given by classical philosophy, by the Stoics and by Cicero, robbing of its scandal the message of the resurrection reunion following the inescapable fact of the cross.

It is here that we come up against the second obstacle, which is a historical one. Over at least the last two centuries conflict, and not the common good, has served as the interpretative model for the history of societies. Different classes have opposing interests and values. Inter-personal evolution is marked by aggressiveness. Identity and relationships cannot be achieved without going through this stage. For anyone who says that human nature is not based on competition, as the appearances might suggest, there is only one further step to take, and that is easily done. From that point, nature itself seems to be a cultural interpretation which can only be put forward among a variety of others. Man is born with a polymorphous nature. It cannot be defined apart from the particular word which may be addressed and communicated to him. In that case, natural law would be a cultural option which refused to pass for what it was, with a content which inevitably encouraged a degree of clericalism. It would be seen as all the more restrictive because it concealed its theological background, presenting as the result of a rational analysis what was in fact an interpretation of the creative Word of God. Nature, then, would be thought to have connotations of creation. But in that case, natural law would have no more claim to general acceptance by non-believers than the Word of faith.

Thus a political theology based on natural law comes up against the theology of the cross and the sociology of conflict. It seems to be handicapped here by a certain static quality, since it seeks to remind man that he has a nature to respect when in fact he has a history to undergo. However, this kind of theology has the twofold advantage of rejecting any attempt at marginalization and aiming not only at a separatist culture but also at the rediscovery of communication and a community.

A second example of transition is provided by political theologies concerned with possible developments rather than with natural data. Here everything is turned upside down. Nature is no longer an indication: it is the future which holds the promise. Creativity replaces creation. God is essentially the one who teaches man to challenge his destiny and make it history. Man must go against all the observances which dehumanize him. The texts and the biblical histories exist to incite all men to this exodus courage, of which the earthly resurrection of Jesus Christ is the universal climax in the New Testament. Here, too, there are political theologies with a universalistic emphasis, since all men of all societies, and not just believers, are invited to live out this transcendence towards the future which has replaced the permanence of nature as the foundation of the majority of contemporary political theologies. Such theologies are more suited to the present time, when alienations and exploitations weigh more heavily than arguments in terms of nature, the negativeness of which is all too likely to prove yet one more burden to bear. We can thus understand how the message of contemporary political theologies can be focused on liberation from conditions of alienation rather than on respect for natural data.

Here too, however, we must ask whether the biblical texts are not used simply as illustrations of a movement which does not have its roots in them, but draws its strength from the future which has now superseded nature as a point of reference. The realm of the possible takes the place of respect, exodus that of support, openness that of fidelity. In this case, however, is there not a reversal of values without any real meta-textual existence on the theological level? Furthermore, the historical level becomes polarized in terms of the one tomorrow, the remembrance of which casts shadows on the past and robs the present of its value. Hence there is a risk that humanity will find its hope revealed as both a refusal and a void. In a later chapter, we shall see in more detail how many contemporary political theologies have gradually taken account of these risks, and how they have sought to alleviate them by paying more attention to the three dimensions of human existence, practising a remembrance of the past and a grasp of the present as well as a hope for the future. That is why I personally find that the best model for moving from the texts to life is provided by a theology of analogy. The biblical stories are analogies which speak for all human history. More specific than an ideal nature, less empty than a challenge to destiny, they show how God acts in history. The analogy has a difficulty which contrasts with that of the two previous examples. It does not begin from evidence available to all, for example concern for a common good or a rejection of slavery, nature or revolution. It begins from stories as specific as, for example, the conflicts between twelve tribes of Aramaean origin, or the situation of a minority subject to historical pressure and mindful of its crucified Lord.

The starting point of the analogy is terribly circumstantial and narrow. However, just as a small mirror can reflect the whole sun, so analogy aims to illuminate all of life by means of circumscribed histories. Of course there is not enough information or systematic reflection on which to build a political doctrine. Analogy remains a light which sets out to lighten those who seek to relate the texts to life. Like a mirror, it is concentrated on a single focal point. The light is diffused over different areas, just as the seed is scattered on varied terrain. The transition is still difficult; the mirror must not lose its focus, so that it ceases to illuminate situations, but it must not do more than reflect them. To my mind, however, the decisive advantage of analogy is that it constantly reflects the tension between particular texts and global existence.

Analogy is truly meta-textual. It requires concentration on a particular focal point so as to obtain illumination which is neither banal nor empty, but distinctive while being universal. Analogy amounts to an orientation in two directions: towards the texts, where there is communication from elsewhere by means of stories, and towards life, where the light drives away the shadows and ushers in a dawn. This is what I have tried to achieve by my discussion of revolution in reunions and patience under pressure. Here we really do relate the texts of the Bible, which are the context of our partial knowledge, to life, which is the context in which we resolve to act. 'For now we see in a mirror dimly, but then face to face. Now I know in part; then I shall understand fully, even as I have been fully understood. So faith, hope, love abide, these three; but the greatest of these is love' (I Cor. 13.12f.).

4

Words and Violence

Words and violence in politics

Politics involves words because it calls for an expression of opinion on the part of those who are subjects, not in the sense of being victims of caprice and powerlessness, but as agents in a corporate process and institution. If almost all modern states have at least a nominally democratic regime, for all that this may be merely a facade, a rubber stamp on decisions taken by others, and face the temptation to woo support from the voters, this is certainly because democracy affirms the active role of all its subjects. Politics also involves words because those who maintain or seek power use persuasion to acquire it, explanation to exercise it and argumentation to keep it. Corporate decisions are made through words. Words abolish the isolation of the subordinate and the autocrat. They break down the barriers of ignorance and secrecy, by opening up the dialogue which constantly puts into effect the contract between political subjects and their representatives, between their various opinions and concerns, and finally between what is desirable, what is possible and what is decided on. Words prevent politics from being the dispossession of some and the privilege of others: instead it becomes a sharing, corporate deliberation. Those who use words are in search of an alliance, and any theology of God the Word who seeks an alliance with mankind will insist on the essential presence of words in politics, since words are neither 'ideological' trickery or 'idealistic' chatter, but a link which creates a mutual bond.

However, politics also involves violence, that is, if violence can be understood in positive terms as the force which is indispensable for putting into effect what would otherwise remain in the realm of longing and regret. First of all, therefore, I do not propose to contrast words used in deliberation with brutal violence. I must, however, make the point that political words are weak, apart from a concern to transform them into action or to win respect for them. Furthermore, it is of the essence of politics to seize power in order to be able to control forces, whether these are the forces of opposition and dispersion, or of rejection and dissolution. Politics can comprise a violence which is accepted because its legitimation, at least in principle, is provided by the words of a social contract. Hence we need to draw a distinction between illegitimate violence, which flares up when communication by words becomes impossible, and amounts to an act of vengeance pure and simple, and legitimate violence, which is based on words which are known and recognized, i.e. institutional words, and are part of the administration of justice. Political institutions intervene in the realm between vengeance and justice; they are governed by an agreed form of words which recognizes that the violence which they administer is legitimate.

Vengeance and justice

The distinction between vengeance and justice can be found in the Bible. It can be found, for example, in the Old Testament, where we see a contrast between the terrifying vengeance which Lamech, the descendant of Cain who is worse than his ancestor, intends to wreak on his people ('Wives of Lamech, hearken to what I say: I have slain a man for wounding me, a young man for striking me. If Cain is avenged sevenfold, truly Lamech seventy-sevenfold' (Gen. 4.23f.)), and the judicial enactment which will protect Cain who, though guilty, from henceforth enjoys the protection of an institutional sign ('The Lord said, "Not so! If anyone slays Cain, vengeance shall be taken on him sevenfold." And the Lord put a mark on Cain, lest any who came upon him should kill him' (Gen. 4.15). Lamech vents his personal anger without any attempt at conversation. Cain survives, thanks to a form of violence which is recognized as a legitimate protection. Similarly, in the great political passage in the letter to the Romans, we can see Paul forbidding individuals to take vengeance wrongfully by resorting to violence ('Beloved, never avenge yourselves', Rom. 12.19). On the contrary, they are to recognize the legitimacy of judicial violence, since this is exercised by the magistrates, who are God's servants and God's instruments. They have been appointed for this function ('He is the servant of God to execute his wrath on the wrongdoer', Rom. 13.4). So violence changes colour depending on whether it is exercised by the individual, as an inability to get the better of his resentment, or politically, as a capacity to impose justice on the wicked. Hence politics will differ from the inter-personal sphere in being the realm in which violence can be used without incurring the charges either of lacking love or of anticipating God's future judgment. We should take note that in the two texts which I have quoted, this legitimate violence is retributive punishment for the wicked and a recompense to the good (indeed, in the case of Cain, the guilty party is protected against the vengeful passion of individuals). This violence is in no way justified simply by the possession of power or by the relentless need for action. It is used to good ends. These two texts express the situation of dependence in which legitimate violence is in accord with law, on the premise that the authorities have been instituted by God: 'The Lord put a sign on Cain' (Gen. 4.15); 'For there is no authority except from God, and those that exist have been instituted by God' (Rom. 13.1). We should not take this to mean that the political authorities are to recognize God, or that they express his will by the mere fact of their existence. Their present judicial function should correspond to the future function of God's judgment. So these texts envisage neither a political theocracy nor a divinization of the state, but the legitimation of authority by its present judicial acts. So it is that retributive justice is established simply to thwart the disorder brought about by vengeance and its abuses. Vengeance constitutes an indefinite impulse towards destruction, whereas retributive justice is a necessary institution, albeit limited by the fact that it is distributive and provides protection, though without taking the place of God who alone determines, pardons and saves. We see how the Bible puts us on our guard on the one hand against the unleashing of human anger which, by its impatience and arrogance, increases the evil already in circulation, but on the other hand warns us against any anticipation of divine judgment by human justice, which is itself under an obligation to observe rules made to punish and protect, to encourage and maintain.

So in the Bible, which is the book of the Word, a place is also found for violence, when this does not contradict the Word. On the contrary, it is used to ensure that the Word has its double effect of nourishing and warning. It is because the Bible takes account of the need for violence that it is not wedded to the pious and empty vows of moralism and idealism. At the exodus from Egypt, Pharaoh's oppression and hard-heartedness need to be overcome by a strong hand and a stretched-out arm. Similarly, in all the accounts of the resurrection of Jesus Christ, we hear of hostile powers who have been unmasked, stripped and fettered. According to the Bible, it is in this resistance to the cumulative lures of wickedness and rancour that violence proves to be both legitimate and necessary. We can see this better if we note the way in which the sign put on Cain prevents vendetta, or listen to the pressing exhortation made by St Paul to the Christians of Rome. Although they are dangerously close to the shadow of Nero, they are not to fear political authority but to submit to it, 'not only to avoid God's wrath but also for the sake of conscience' (Rom. 13.5).

The object is in fact to obtain from man something that is always most difficult for him: free submission, whole-hearted consent, obedience without abdication or fear. Conscience has to intervene. Etymologically, conscience is shared knowledge, the common recognition that henceforth man shares with God the need to use violence legitimately, so that the Word will not be frustrated by evil acts and also so that these evil acts do not serve as a good opportunity for those who, believing themselves to be good, in fact prove to be worse than the wicked in their vengeance. Here, then, violence is not the temptation offered to the covetousness of power, but the bridle put on the neck of those who claim impunity. It is not an institutional veil, to disguise the bad conscience of vengeance or envy as legitimacy or legality. It is the acceptance in good conscience of the rule of the authorities instituted for the good, for those who acknowledge a just God also acknowledge the need for a just authority, in the midst of the unjust powers of the earth. It is there to see that each one has his due: in connection with taxes, revenue, respect, honour (Rom. 13.7). Such language seems shocking today when we often look resentfully on any constraint as oppression, and when we dream of a form of politics which will have become so adult and so unanimous that it will be able to do away with constraint. However, such sentiments are exaggerated and such a dream is an illusion. Precisely because it speaks politically without dreaming idealistically, the Bible recognizes the protective function of violence, at the same time knowing all too well about its devastating temptation.

So we have to distinguish between two forms of violence. One only heeds the anger of the individual or the group, bent on vengeance or exploitation; the other is a legitimate protection against anger and applies itself to just retribution. However, it is not enough to make this distinction on a theoretical level, to assure that there is no protection against a confused way of living. Politics cannot be separated from the interpersonal as neatly as I may have seemed to suggest, and the one who acts as 'magistrate' will not find it easy to put aside personal emotions and social position. He will administer justice in accordance with his temperament and above all his allegiances. Under the cover of justice, aimed at protecting the guilty from blind anger, it is anger that he will execute. He will act as though his institutional position were a guarantee of the legitimacy of his authority, whereas the just exercise of this authority is what gives his institutional position its validity. The distinction between vengeance and justice, then, cannot be made in terms of the degree of violence involved. The decisive factor is the goal which is pursued, in the one case to find satisfaction, in the other to hinder and protect. Vengeance does away with words in order to sate itself with anger. By contrast, justice restores the Word, so that little by little the disruptive effects of anger may cease. The judgment of justice cannot be content with supervision and punishment exercised mutely and repressively, putting the victim well away. It seeks to bring the guilty under the protection offered him by the law, so that little by little he may be restored to the world of words, the sharing that is constitutive of the society from which his 'wickedness' has cut him off. As long as justice fails to pursue this course until reintegration is achieved, it remains social vengeance, ill disguised under the dignity of an institution.

Violence and lies

Because of what we have seen, it is impossible to be content with banning individual violence and legitimating political violence within the state organization. We need to go further and see how and why this move from the word towards violence takes place, so that we can consider how violence can once again give place to the word. Justice is neither isolated nor absolute. It is a necessary institutional element, the centre of the context in which it is set, flanked on the one hand by the roots of violence, and on the other by a return to verbal communication. Nor is the state a separate body, with an authority that is above all suspicion. It is a necessary organizational element at the centre of the context in which it is set, flanked on the one hand by conflicts and war, and on the other by a return to negotiations and even more to those reconciliations which bear the name of peace. Violence is not the decisive verdict of justice. It is a restraining, protective, necessary element at the centre of the context in which it is set, flanked on the one hand by disengagement and on the other by pacification. So violence only exists in tension with words which now disguise it and provoke it, now accept it and appease it. We need to go back this far if we are not to be content with an empty verbal contrast between legitimate violence and illegitimate violence, which are differentiated only by the fact that the former is exercised by the one who holds power whereas the latter is always directed illegally against him. This criterion is certainly not unimportant, as we have seen, since the task of existing political power is to prevent the pursuit of vengeance by individuals. However, it is inadequate if the power in possession confines itself to reprimanding, without listening or pacifying, in other words, if it uses violence solely to sweep away the words which provoke it. In that case, although it is there to defend and protect, it perpetuates itself by oppression and destruction. Without recourse to shared words, even legitimate, institutional violence turns into tyranny.

We have to accept that violence may begin when communication through words breaks down. In any case, this happens in the typical story told in the Bible of the first murder. Cain becomes angry and miserable because God has preferred the sacrifice of his brother, Abel the shepherd, and not his own, that of Cain the husbandman. However, this curious disparity is not presented as the real source and cause of Cain's violence. In that case it would be God who was really at fault. The time when words break down and violence enters the scene is when Cain refuses to listen to the God who is speaking to him, attacks Abel and kills him. The word is an act of confidence in the usefulness of communication in making peace. Greek philosophy is built on the confidence that if one defines the words used without misunderstanding, one can reject the pessimism of tragedy, which describes the captivity of free individuals in the toils of destiny, and the scepticism of the sophists, who use words to bewitch and influence but not to illustrate and convince. Philosophy is confidence in the capacity of words to educate and exert political influence, and, if they are correctly defined, to establish relationships of law and justice among men.

That is why the lie is the first and most poisonous source of injustice. The lie is a use of words which destroys the confidence one should be able to place in them. It supports words and uses them, but does so essentially by emptying them of the element of communication which they were called on to initiate or restore. The lie is born of stratagem and engenders mistrust. It is first of all the lie (and not pride, or hate, much less sensuality) that the Bible sees as the work of the crafty serpent, who will later become the divider, the accuser, the murderer, the tempter, Satan, the devil. He utters lies and makes them so attractive that they sound like the truth. In so doing he gnaws away at the word from within. He continues to make it seem attractive, but he empties it of its substance.

By keeping to this theological and symbolic representation of the fall in the Bible,[20] Kant was the philosopher who laid most stress on this first destruction of the word by the lie. This happens when it rules out any possibility of exchange and puts violence, i.e. a lack of trust in words, in its place. It is wrong to go on talking if the words are uttered only to tranquillize and to deceive. So from now on words appear as radical evil, the root of the darkness within man and between men, since men are inexplicably led to convert its truth into cleverness. They are then guided not by truth but by the interest that they may eventually derive from it. All Kant's moral and religious philosophy centres on this inexplicable degeneration of words, made to bring clarity and trust, but put over in such a way that they encourage the pollution of life and the separation of men. Kant sees real salvation only in a second decision, as free and inexplicable as the first, to speak the truth from now on, without any qualification, and whatever the circumstances might be which would lead a man to suggest whatever was pleasant, charitable or profitable. Kant's intransigence in the categorical observation of principles is proportionate to his recognition of the possible perversion of every word uttered with lying intent. The element in this rigorism that we need to retain is the capacity that all words have to deceive when (to put it in biblical terms) they are born of the serpent and not of God, and when God can use only the violence of his anger to destroy man's false confidence in the serpent. For God's expulsion of man from the garden of Eden is an angry reaction against the serpent's lies at man's expense. He is seduced, deceived, hunted, but from henceforth under protection in this world, where violence is born of the deceits of the word.

That, I think, is the first source of violence, the one that I have called the Kantian source. The word has become a lie. It can no longer be counted on. Men can no longer trust any preaching, instruction, legislation, advice, liberalization or socialization which remains in the realm of theory and is not put into practice. Violence is a mute reaction which henceforward goes its own way. The fear of being cheated gives force to violence. When lambs are being slaughtered, it is best to advance like a wolf. Of course, in this brief account of the reasons for violence, which stems from the deceptive character of words, I have argued as though the situation began with someone else's lie and not with one's own. I do, however, think that there is justification for proceeding in this way, recognizing the inexplicable presence of the serpent in God's good creation, the prelude to man's free sin. Violence stems from lies told to us. The lies which we ourselves utter are not violent in themselves, they are deceitful and wicked. Violence develops when all confidence in words has been lost and when attack seems the only way of getting a response.

Violence and injustice

We have now come close to the second source of violence, which I would prefer to call the Hegelian source. Violence does not only develop when words prove deceitful. It is also associated with the realization of hopes. Kant identified the lie, the abandonment of the truth for self-interest, as the root of evil. Hegel located the origin of violence in history, in conflict, risking life for recognition. Here violence is no longer a lapse into mistrust, but a cry for attention. It is courage in the face of the threat of the anonymity of slavery. It is a courage which involves patience and sacrifice for one's heritage. It has to make use of the chains which gag it. At this point, Hegel recognizes the need for stratagem and even lies if there is going to be any understanding of what comes from the bad side of history, that is, not the side of truth, autonomy, transparency and confidence, as in Kant, but the side of obscurity, dependence, bravery and conflict. Here, then, the source of violence is not so much the abandonment of words because they are false, but a progress towards words through the barriers of injustice. Before we can have confidence in words, we have to find ourselves in a position to use them, and to achieve that we have to dethrone those who deny our right to exist in the name of their privileges. For Kant, the lie was an obstacle; here it can become the means to an end. However, here too violence can only be a means of transition towards shared living. Neither conflict nor violence are tests, incitements or ends in themselves. They need to be overtaken by an understanding of developments, but this can only come about at the risk of confrontation and fragmentation. Here, too, the goal is the true use of words, but this goal is not arrived at, as in Kant, through a personal, radical and instantaneous conversion from lies to the truth, but by a corporate progression, the experience of which is as tragic as its necessity is logical, from conflict towards the totality; from injustice towards liberty and equality.

I have used Kant and Hegel as philosophical models for illustrating two possible sources of violence which are often confused. First, there is the violence of the person who falls back on his fury and resentment because he no longer believes in words, which he sees as being tainted with falsehood. In his violence, there is that sense of being cheated which can be found at the root of all bitterness. The man who is cheated turns to his anger, because he has decided not to go on with the useless business of talking and listening. This violence founded on a rejection of words is very difficult to combat. Its past cuts it off from all the future. It cannot and will not change because it has already experienced both hope and its collapse. It loftily affirms that it will not be caught out twice over the stupid business of truth, justice or love. It is a murderous violence which refuses to be taken in by those who speak fair

words. Such closed-in violence is haunted by memory. That
is without doubt why Kant thinks in terms of a return to the
truth which is as radical and disinterested as the resort to lies
was a matter of self-interest. He does not attempt any gentle
form of teaching, any argument, for example, from the human
destruction which sets such violence in motion. The past has
become inexplicably corrupt and shadowy. The very fact that
this free fall of man from truth to the lie is utterly inexplicable,
in no way a voluntary choice (since passions or social injustice
or some hidden destiny can be no more than a pretext for this
fall, rather than its true cause) seems to Kant proof evident
that the contrary choice, of the truth against the lie, is also
completely free and possible. The force of this argument is that
it rejects the inevitability of violence and affirms that man can
change at any time, of his own free will, if he so desires. In a
similar fashion, at the beginning of his work Sartre affirmed
that no situation can ever be seen as a determining factor, and
that completely new situations can develop out of previous
circumstances. Instead of a fatal progression of violence, we
have situations of violence from which anyone can emerge to
find a new life by deciding to return to the truth, that is to say,
to words which give men confidence. They will not expect the
least personal advantage or the least social recompense from
this decision, because they will decide for the truth by conviction, and not because they expect to gain any benefit. The
rigorist and the voluntarist have nothing to gain but the freedom
of personal action.

Nevertheless, there is something abstract about this high-
flown and pure description of conversion from the lie to the
truth, from destiny to liberty. The person envisaged here
would seem to have kept his balance at the very moment of his
worst enslavement in fury and rancour. For all his violence, he
remains sufficiently himself to be able to regain all of a sudden
his dignity and sociability. By rejecting any alternative cause
for the wreck of his words through deceit or his liberty through
determination, this approach runs the risk of depriving him
of any means of escaping from the wreck. He is at the bottom

of a well and the only rope by which he can get out must be provided by his own decision. I think that this description of violence as a deliberate act of defiance is an essential one, but I think that violence is also a somewhat dubious step in a quest for victory. Hence the importance of Hegel's analyses, which are less moral and voluntaristic than those of Kant or the early Sartre, but much more historical and instructive. For violence is not just a matter of liberty being taken over by the lie. It is also a matter of captivity seeking the prospect of liberty. Liberty does not depend only on my resolute and altruistic determination to obey. It also depends on whether I can clear any way among others, against them and with them. Only through their acceptance will my violence gradually come once again to take the form of words which bring knowledge and agreement instead of having to be instruments of trickery and temporizing. Community and peace are characterized by the agreement of free men; they are the ultimate horizon of a history which has previously seen every possible manifestation of violence: anxiety and fear, anger and indignity, conflict and disunity. At this point, however, we can ask a question which is diametrically opposed to the one raised earlier. Does not such a long process of evolution, which in other respects is so problematical, justify all the violence which individuals suffer and on which they founder? Is it not a necessary part of developments? Furthermore, does not this process excuse individuals from making a voluntary and immediate personal decision? If violence has a place not only in lies but in the global and universal struggle for recognition and justice, is there not a risk that responsibility for this violence will always be foisted on to others? By the same token, does not that also relieve us of our own responsibility and destroy the hope that one day we might bring an end to our violence, lies and injustice by rejecting them ourselves? In taking corporate form, violence becomes endemic, whereas in the earlier instance it ran the risk of remaining abstract because it was expressed in personal terms. Consequently, these two analyses are fated to be complementary. Where there is no personal involvement in the truth, confidence never takes the place of violence; one power simply succeeds its predecessor. Besides, the truth can never remain a matter of individual sincerity. That will never transform the conditions under which groups recognize one another, according to power structures, within which liberty and equality need to be realized if brotherhood is not to be a meaningless title for a disembodied ideal.

We really ought to explore a number of other sources of violence: fear, when it does not find an outcome either in negotiation or in flight, and when it makes man, like animals, into bundles of desperate aggressiveness; envy, and passion generally, when men want immediately and absolutely something that they are too lazy to acquire otherwise or cannot have anyway; cruelty which, set on its objectives, does not tolerate any resistance. . . But it was not my concern here to analyse the different origins of violence, of this desire which turns into rape when reality does not submit to the word of its command. I have simply chosen two examples to show how the word turns into violence, perhaps because mistrust has been introduced by lies, or perhaps because free men have rebelled against humiliation. In these two instances, perhaps more clearly than in others, we can see how violence does not so much contrast with words as eclipse them, and how men are required not to condemn it, but to rescue it from madness and its disaster. Violence is most often a means to an end, the words which it cannot formulate.

Violence and the cross

Now, however, we must return to the biblical scene. Violence is constant in this book of the Word. In effect, it takes both forms: that of the lie, which leads to bitterness, and of the competitive struggle for recognition, which provokes wars. If the Bible seeks to express the terms of a covenant, that is to say, trust between God and man, between man and man, and between man and nature, it might be argued that its content is a long history of violence perpetrated and endured. Man does not believe in the goodness of the Word of God in his situation. He breaks the covenant by mistrust: in the real world which has been given to him by God's goodness, he prefers another, better, imaginary world which has been suggested by the serpent's lie. So it would be better to call this story a tale of lack of trust in the Word rather than an account of the fall. This last word always seems to stress a mythological explanation for the present state of humanity, fallen, fragile and mortal, whereas the tenor of the story is that men should believe in the goodness of the Word of God and not mistrust it. Here violence derives from an alternative which is put forward as an alternative to trust. Perhaps God is simply forgetful: his goodness towards the world and particularly towards his own people could have been greater. Perhaps God is simply a tyrant who imposes his law and his promises, who requires obedience and attention. In both these cases God is suspected of lying, and this suspicion plunges man into bitterness and prompts vengeance. Vengeance here takes the form first of accusation and then of doubt. It engenders a solitude which is exactly the opposite of blessing. Those who are abandoned see violence as a bottomless pit. The dividing line of the lie reaches a peak in the biblical figures where faces are hidden, withdrawn or turned away and the truth is overcome by the evidence of dereliction: this happens often with Abraham and David, with Jeremiah and Job, and above all with Jesus Christ.

However, the second form of violence, the struggle for recognition, is even more evident in the Bible. That explains why this book of reconciliation and peace contains the accounts of so many wars. These are fratriarchal wars, waged among an excessive number of heirs for a single promise. Anyone who does not fight is dispossessed, even if he was the first-born in terms of descent and inheritance. There are wars of conquest, in which those who do not fight do not take possession of what has in any case been given to them by divine promise. There are wars to which all the tribes are summoned, which are as imperative in their way as confessions of faith, without being imperialistic. There are dynastic wars in which the two kingdoms,

Israel in the north and Judah in the south, which in due
course part company, serve as a warning to each other while
vying with one another. Finally, there are the apocalyptic and
eschatological wars in which God himself adopts the cause of
his people who from now on are dependent and dispersed, with
no autonomous life of their own. There are always wars; there
is always violence. This is not because the God of the Old
Testament has a disconcerting tendency to resemble the warrior
gods of his time, but because the Bible confirms the story we
have told of violence used to further the struggle for recognition,
so that the Word may be given to all and neither God nor his
people may be isolated in a mutual oblivion which neither
unites them in a covenant nor brings them mutual peace.

However, it was wrong to write 'mutual' in the last sentence,
as though the Bible told of a progressive mutual agreement
between God and humanity, and as though the biblical history
was a matter of the on-going liberation of man by God and of
God by man. The Bible does not talk in this way. It uses the
word redemption, so that we should not think only in terms of
liberation, which implies that we are the ones who do the
liberating, unless it is qualified by another more basic word,
salvation. In fact redemption is God's decisive blow when sin
triumphs, and when there is no chance of liberation through
mutual recognition on the part of both man and God. Man
does not recognize God and God does not want to violate his
failure in recognition. Furthermore, God must either renounce
man, or take vengeance on him, or take on himself the violence
which man has done to him. So there are three different ways
of interpreting the cross as the ultimate violence which arises
from the sin which is an absence of reciprocity. It can appear as
solidarity and renunciation, a merciful yet impotent combination of God's kindness with man's sorrow. It can also be
understood as remorse and bitterness, the vengeful accusation
which God makes against human ingratitude and deafness.
In the former case the cross is the memorial of a martyr, in the
latter it is the tomb of a prophet. But the story of the empty
tomb has been included in the gospels precisely in order to

counter these two possibilities, to show that the cross is neither impotence nor vengeance, but violence which God takes on himself in the death of his well-beloved Son, when there is a rift between him and humanity. Thus redemption achieves what mutual liberation will not. In this redemption, the saviour carries the burden and pays the price for the one who is saved. By concentrating violence on the saviour, this redemption puts an end to the war for recognition, not by renouncing it or by bowing down under misfortune; not by denouncing it or by perpetuating evil; but in disarming the evildoer. At this point lie and conflict reach the limit. But at precisely this point they are taken on by the one who is called Word, truth and peace; that is, his love makes him concerned for their victory and frees us from anxiety that they may be thwarted.

I have stressed strongly that redemption is not a reciprocal affair, because anyone who seeks to maintain man's honour, by stressing how he is involved in the struggle for recognition to the bitter end, has the misfortune to mar the joy which he receives from the gift of his liberation. Such an attitude suggests that there is no stopping point in the infinite progression of pretensions and deceptions, of struggles and domination, that there is no centre where God himself converts this accumulated violence into the gift of the word. Now the cross is both the word suppressed by violence and violence arrested for the word.

However, once this stopping point has been seen as a decisive event which changes personal and universal history, the reciprocity has to be restored. Because of the cross, human attempts are no longer oriented on an unattainable ideal but based on an actual achievement, and this includes attempts on the part of men who do not see any decisive meaning in the cross of Jesus Christ or would prefer to see it as an illustration, a model of sorrow or accusation. On the basis of the cross, the way towards reciprocity is not an illusion but a possible pursuit and a new beginning.

As we shall see in the next chapter, contemporary political theologies have reverted to the cross, after seeing the resurrection as the way towards new possibilities. In so doing they have recognized that the cross sets the Word in its substratum, violence, and that any words which do not come to grips with violence remain at its mercy. Without the word of resurrection, no hope is opened up, but without the violence of the cross, there is no real hope at all.

5

From the Promise of the Resurrection
to the Memory of the Cross

A strange sequence

In this chapter I shall seek to analyse and assess the various
contemporary political theologies which in fact began by
celebrating the future, the possible, symbolized by resurrection,
and then went on to meditate on life, the past, reality, symbolized by the cross. However, the chapter title and the
sequence remain strange. We ought always to move, without
constantly looking behind us, from the impasse of the cross to
the Easter breakthrough, following the sequence of St Paul's
exclamation: 'Who shall bring any charge against God's elect?
It is God who justifies; who is to condemn? It is Christ Jesus,
who died, who was raised from the dead, who is at the right
hand of God, who indeed intercedes for us' (Rom. 8.33f.
RSV margin).

In the Bible the deteiminative sequence is a unilinear one:
from the cross to the resurrection. This is the decisive point
which distinguishes biblical faith from the alternatives which,
taken together, are characteristic of all religions and the
majority of ideologies. They complement one another, are
elements in a cycle, and their order can be reversed: death and
life, night and day, sorrow and happiness, disappearance and
reappearance. Life is swallowed up by death and then gives
rise to new life. According to the great and ultimately timeless
cycles which are characterized by the seasons and by nature, by
civilizations and history, mythologies and the unconscious,

man is born to lament and laments that he has been born. The Bible, which is concerned with events and eschatology, takes an opposite line to these symbolic and repetitive alternatives. The Bible tells of decisive moments, the 'once-for-allness' of which may be recalled, reactualized and relived, but never repeated. There is only one exodus towards one kingdom, one cross followed by one Easter. Otherwise, we would have abandoned the incarnation of God in terrestrial history for the representation of the divine in archaic or utopian imagination. This 'once-for-allness' of events which bring accomplishment and revelation, which never repeat themselves, has nothing to do with a naïve religious imperialism or an abstract universalism. It indicates that we have left the ever-repeated cycles of nature to come up against those turning points, those irreversible junctures, which God puts in the web of the world, and which are best described as acts of grace: 'There is one body and one Spirit, just as you were called to the one hope that belongs to your call, one Lord, one faith, one baptism; one God and Father of us all, who is above all and through all and in all' (Eph. 4.4–6). The word 'one' here does not signify 'imperialistic', or 'synthetic', but 'unique'. For anything that is not unique dissolves in the incessant repetition of nature, whether materialist or idealist, secularized or divinized, unless it comes face to face with God. God is not the One, the common denominator of the many. God is Unique, the one who is before all and for all.

Thus to talk of life and death, death and life, is not the same as to believe in a fundamentally new order, from the cross to the resurrection of Jesus Christ. So because contemporary political theologies have departed from the usual pattern and moved from the future aspect of the resurrection towards the remembrance of the cross, the first question we have to ask is why they have come to correct themselves in this way. In this sense, are they not reactive theologies, using the word in the sense in which Nietzsche contrasts reactive, mistrustful, contorted, with active, spontaneous and positive?[21] Do they not perhaps have a belated concern to correct their first mistakes while lacking a clear dialectic which is capable of linking the cross and its remembrance with the resurrection and its victory? In our examination of contemporary political theologies we shall not evade these essential questions. At the same time, however, we can see how such theologies follow one of the basic developments experienced by the first Christian community. It too, having experienced the glare of Easter, which heightened its expectation of the imminent return of Jesus the Christ and the end of the first creation, returned towards the cross. We can see how the cross is still remembered and forms a permanent element in Christian life at the point when Paul says to the Corinthians, who have been lit up by the newness of Easter and the gifts of the spirit: 'I decided to know nothing among you except Christ Jesus and him crucified' (I Cor. 2.2). In this case, the rediscovery of the remembrance of the cross will be less a correction than a deeper understanding of the promise of Easter. We shall see which of these two interpretations is preferable, and whether contemporary political theologies are teetering on a tightrope or whether they arrive at a convincing understanding of the truth.

Political theologies and the diversity of their sociological roots

A variety of titles have been used to describe the theologies which have proliferated over the past ten years or so, following in the wake of dogmatic hermeneutical theologies, as I indicated in the first chapter. There are theologies of hope, theologies of revolution, theologies of liberation, theologies of insurrection or, to group them in the contexts which have given rise to them: black theologies, African theologies, anti-sexist theologies, socialist theologies, theologies of development (which became theologies of dependence when development proved to be both paternalist and illusory), and so on.

We have to acknowledge that it is difficult to attach any great importance to the diversity of these titles. Many arise from the addition of the adjective 'theological' to a variety of situations and the hopes and despairs, fears and even resentments to which they give rise. The domination from which liberation is sought is varied: economic domination, bound up with exploitation and largely connected with property; political domination, bound up with imperialism and for the most part concerned with power; cultural domination, bound up with displacement and for the most part concerned with identity; and psychological domination, bound up with alienation and for the most part concerned with the emotions. The liberations will not be the same in each case. One can see a variety of conflicts which have as their common denominator a protest directed against the existing order of things and look to a rebellion to change them. If one follows the contexts of the revolutionary movements analysed by Marcuse in his various works, it is also necessary to note that these contexts are multiple. They can be found among the peoples of the Third World, who are dependent on the industrialized countries, whether the latter have free economies or a centralized socialist system. They can also be found among the poor and the marginal members of affluent or developing societies, and among the younger generation in the same societies who, while not themselves the direct victims of poverty and exploitation, are disturbed at the bleak prospects and above all the meaninglessness of the cycle of mass production, mass consumption and mass communication which confronts them. These very different origins explain why so-called political theologies have in fact arisen in two very different areas: in those countries which have a high level of economic dependence and a developed critical conscience (essentially in Latin America),[22] and in countries with considerable economic capacity but little social cohesion (essentially in West Germany).[23] Thus from the start we have to deal with two sources: the suffering of those who feel that they are being exploited, and the suffering of those who feel that they occupy a marginal position. Of the two groups, the former will tend to feel that the latter are indulging more or less in a luxury, whereas the latter will feel that the aggressiveness of the former is essentially a consequence of their situation.

However, there is no point in laying too much stress here on the different contexts of these different theologies. To do that would be to risk regarding them as being essentially reactions which reflect the different sociologies of their situations, whereas they seek to be the active theological catalysts for these situations. So let us attempt, rather, to examine their dominant theological features and to see why they all regard the resurrection as a new beginning and an inauguration of the future.

The resurrection, the inauguration of the future of the world

In earlier theologies, God was either a transcendent Word bursting in on the world with its restricted horizons and its false sense of self-sufficiency to bring about the salvation promised to faith, or a language the truth and profundity of which can be verified by human experience, incomparable with the other languages in which man makes himself at home. In both these approaches, which I have called dogmatic and hermeneutical theologies, God is above all a message addressed to man to win him over to the liberty of faith.

If I understand them aright, so-called political theologies lay stress on God in another way. They see him as the one who intervenes in the world, challenging its order and announcing its deliverance. They are political, because they are chiefly concerned with the histories of societies, with their present alienations, future liberations and ultimate reconciliations. And they are theological, because they contrast with a God who may be called upon to guarantee and hallow the *status quo*, another God whose dynamism is subversive and whose work here has only just begun and has yet to be accomplished. Thus these theologies bring to the fore the challenging, prophetic, 'apocalyptic' and eschatological pole of Christianity as a counter-balance to the established, institutional, dogmatic, 'Constantinian' pole which they believe to have been dominant in the thought and practice of the Christian church during the course of its history. We can see how at this point these theo-logies meet up with the new interpretation given by many

Communists today to the classic condemnation of religion by
Marxism. They argue that this condemnation is a useless and
mystifying digression. In fact, they distinguish between two
types of religion. One is conservative. It provides a legitimation
for those who exercise power within a terrestrial hierarchy
which they believe to be divinely instituted, and it comforts the
poor by pacifying them with the expectation of a heavenly
kingdom which will compensate for all that has gone before.
This religion is bad: its structures are idealistic and it has an
oppressive effect. However, there could also be another religion,
or rather another possible role for religion which Marxists (at
least for the time being) believe to be valuable. This religion is
an expression of protest and subversion; it is constantly on the
move, and in fact is revolutionary. In this context we may
quote at length the famous passage from Marx of which the
last sentence is often the only part to be remembered: 'Religious
distress is at the same time the expression of real distress and
also the protest against real distress. Religion is the sigh of the
oppressed creature, the heart of a heartless world, just as it is
the spirit of spiritless conditions. It is the opium of the people.'[24]

Beyond question, then, there are points of contact, or at least
similarities, between political theologies which set out to
present a God who disrupts human history, and the distinctions
which certain Marxists have begun to draw in their assessments
of the historical effects of religion, and above all of Christianity.
At the same time, however, we need to raise two sets of
questions. The first concerns political theologies: do they think
that God favours one side in the historical class struggle? Do
they not risk conferring their blessing on revolution rather than
the forces of law and order, thus becoming the prisoners of one
camp and forgetting the universality of sin and grace? The
second concerns Marxism: for how long, in what circumstances,
and in what contexts, can it give religion a positive function?
In the Marxist perspective, the recognition of a positive
historical contribution does not amount to an ideological
convergence of materialism and idealism (all forms of Christianity being included in the latter category). So even given this

new positive evaluation of religion, how is it possible to avoid charges of tactical opportunism or ideological confusion? There are, then, important connections between political theologies on the one side and Marxist interpretations on the other, even if they differ over the nature of religion. However, the encounter remains a difficult one. Each partner risks losing its central core: theology that of salvation by grace and Marxism that of dialectical materialism.

Still, the essential thing is for political theologies to show that divine transcendence does not signify the removal of God into the realms of idealistic abstraction or subjective inwardness. It points to the upheaval he introduces within human history. Moltmann charges Bultmann with devaluing the transformation of history so that it becomes existential historicity. In other words, for Bultmann the believer is dissociated from the world and finds himself with a direct relationship to the eternal. Moltmann also charges Barth with trivializing history by stressing the fullness of the Christ event which has already taken place to such a degree that its eschatological conclusion will only unveil a reality which is already present, without adding anything substantial to it. Similarly, Gustavo Gutierrez charges classical scholastic theology with presenting itself either as a way to unitive contemplation or as analogical knowledge; in either case it prevents theology from playing its full part in shaping the future of the world. Yet again, Jean-Baptiste Metz undertakes to reverse the anti-modernist tendency of the church's tradition which constantly laments the old days, now gone, when syntheses could still be constructed. By contrast, he puts forward a positive assessment of democratic society, which sets up its own institutions; of critical thought, which puts the affirmations of faith through the crucible of doubt; of the secular world, which is a consequence of the incognito of the incarnation; and above all of the value of research, the appeal to discovery rather than to possession.

I have brought different works together here, since they do not have the same antecedents, nor are they directed against the same opponents. However, what they have in common **is** that they all insist on the possibilities, the deficiencies and the appeals of the future. They give the impression of wanting desperately to demonstrate that the kerygmatic and doxological, patristic and scholastic, traditional and magisterial past of Christianity does not stand in the way of its future. The God who has been and who is, will also continue to be. Here we can recognize two great philosophical influences on these theologians. First, there is that of Hegel, who links the interior and immanent Trinity of God with the exterior and economic Trinity of his manifestation in the growth of the world, so that Hegel's God will only come fully to be at the end of a universal history. Secondly, there is that of Ernst Bloch, who sees a genesis only at the end of what is still in process of happening, thus making hope a principle of utopian thought. However, because Bloch is an atheist, he is not aware of any mythological achievement or any theological guarantee. Intent on emulating these great philosophies of the future, whether trinitarian or utopian, political theologies seek, if not to introduce change into God (which is their temptation), at least to introduce God into change (which is their concern).

This is the reason why they are theologies of resurrection, which is understood as a reactivation of the promise. Different emphases are laid on the central events of the faith, depending on the cultural use which the different theologies make of them. Thus we find an 'apologetic' use of the resurrection: it is the supreme miracle performed to confirm the divinity of Jesus Christ (the nineteenth century thought in this way, but the very same concern can be found today in Pannenberg's christology). There is a 'dogmatic' use: the resurrection marks the juncture and the link between two great movements by which God presents himself to the world: first he empties himself, becomes incarnate, humbles himself, veils himself, is obedient even to the death of the Son on the cross, and thus gives himself to men by the free humiliation of his divinity. Then, irreversibly, there is the movement of exaltation, of resurrection, of ascension, of the dispensation which leads to the reign of the Spirit, the return of the Son and the recapitula-

tion of all things in the Father. In this way God restores and
nurtures men, guiding them from sin to grace and glory
through the free victory of his humanity. The resurrection is
the invisible and invincible return of God to the world and the
reunion of the world with God. Barth's *Dogmatics* adopts this
approach. There is also a kerygmatic usage: the resurrection
sets man's fleshly heart free to announce in the spirit that the
living Christ of faith has succeeded the Jesus who is dead. In
this sense, the death on the cross is already a victory, even
though we do not know that until Pentecost. That is the way
that Bultmann's preaching goes.

Political theologies make a different use of the resurrection.
We might follow Moltmann in calling it 'proleptic' (from the
Greek *prolepsis*, which means anticipation). The resurrection
does not bring an end to Jewish messianic expectations. It
revives them by beginning that recreation of the world of which
the parousia will be the fulfilment; we are those who share in
the inaugurating power of Jesus Christ between the resurrection
and the parousia. He is 'the first-born among many brethren'
(Rom. 8.29), 'the first-born of all creation . . . first-born from
the dead' (Col. 1.15, 18). Thus the resurrection inaugurates
and accelerates the transformation of universal history. It
revives the hope which is the inner tension of the world. It
makes Being a destination to arrive at and not an immovable
foundation. It orients ontology on teleology and not on
archaeology. It makes the church an exodus and not an
institution. Because of the resurrection, the future is the true
expression of reality. Moltmann thinks it significant that for
Greek thought hope is the last illusion to come out of Pandora's
box, whereas Judaeo-Christian thought believes God to leave
traces of his certain promises within history. Thus hope is a
salutary contradiction at the heart of the present. It is impos-
sibly certain. It directs us towards the possibilities of the
future which the resurrection shows to be the consequences of a
development which has already begun, rather than mirages
which constantly disappear from view. That is why, if there is a
priority in faith, it is a primacy of hope. Granted, hope without

faith becomes utopianism, but faith without hope is simply a skeleton without any flesh. The greatest sin, then, is not so much lack of faith as despair, giving up the fight, being imprisoned in sadness, suffocation in the perpetuity of the *status quo*. So Moltmann would want to add to St Anselm's famous phrase 'I believe in order to understand', 'I hope in order to understand'.

At the same time, the aspect of God changes. He is no longer 'epiphanic', appearing in certain circumstances or certain experiences which pierce the opaque screen of phenomena and make them transparent to hidden mysteries, thus affording men access to the divine. God is 'proleptic'. He takes man with him in the anticipation of his promise, so that waiting is no longer a matter of lacking or longing for; it is a time of expectation and action. Moltmann's great book *Theology of Hope* is thus a theology which is built entirely on the resurrection and the parousia, and also a formal description of the change brought about in the concept and countenance of God when his being is his future and his word is the keeping of his promise.

It is easy to see from this why political theologies stress the exodus and liberation. To follow God's new countenance and the resurrection of Jesus Christ is to begin to have expectations of history and to fight against any form of resignation in the present which might indicate the inevitability of future developments. Here we have very different consequences from those of an approach like Albert Schweitzer's, which sees no possibility of a real eschatological conclusion to history because eschatology is a foolish delusion, or an approach like Rudolf Bultmann's, which sees no possibility of eschatology affecting history because it has already been realized in faith. History and eschatology become as it were flesh and spirit. Without historical flesh, eschatology turns into illusion, but without eschatological spirit, history turns into pragmatism. Here everything is measured by the yardstick of openness to the future, of which the resurrection has brought the good news and begun to put it into effect. Moltmann's book is full of phrases which proclaim the opening up of the world to the kingdom, that is to say, to 'exteriorization':[25] 'It is not reflection, recalling man's own subjectivity from its social realization, that brings him back his possibilities and therewith his freedom, but this is done only by the hope which leads him to expend himself and at the same time makes him grasp continually new possibilities from the expected future. . . The expectation of the promised future of the kingdom of God which is coming to man and the world to set them right and create life, makes us ready to expend ourselves unrestrainedly and unreservedly in love and in the work of the reconciliation of the world with God and his future. . . The glory of self-realization and the misery of self-estrangement alike arise from hopelessness in a world of lost horizons. To disclose to it the horizon of the future of the crucified Christ is the task of the Christian church.'[26]

Political theology on the wane

All this is so good, so promising, and there is such a close connection between involvement in the future of society and the confession of faith in a God who changes the world, that we have to ask if such talk is in fact true. It is interesting that all political theologies are suddenly beginning to raise the question themselves, and not before time, considering how long there has been doubt whether progress can be seen in secular history. Theologians have begun to resemble dancers suddenly asking themselves whether they can still walk. Latin-American theologians have seen the failures of avant-garde revolutionaries, now decimated or on the run, resentful and more or less alienated from popular religion. Consequently they now talk in terms of captivity rather than exodus, of dependence rather than liberation, of the pain of God rather than God's hope. In Germany, theologians have gone back to meditating on the cross, a development already implicit in the last sentence of Moltmann's book, quoted above, and in many other passages. The remembrance of the cross is being used as a buttress to support the promise of the resurrection. To play on Moltmann's familiar terms, the cross once again becomes the 'latent realism' without which the 'proleptic tendency' of the resurrection, taken on its own, would degenerate into a mere futurism. For while we look for the parousia and sigh for the final outcome of the resurrection, we also go forward in company with the cross and regard history from its perspective. If God is the one who will be, he is also the one who was, and this permits him from now on to be the one who is.

Conditions are obviously right for this reorientation of contemporary political theology. There have been so many setbacks. Anyone can list them, beginning with the one that personally brought home to him the darkening shadows. In the East there have been the cold war of the Stalinist era and the cruelties practised by socialism with a more human face; in Latin America, fascism has crushed democratic regimes, as in Chile, as well as up-country or urban guerillas, as in Bolivia, Brazil and Argentina; everywhere international solidarity has crumbled when crises, strikes and inflation have threatened individual nations; the ecumenical movement is stagnant because the churches are more concerned about their own inner disintegration than about common progress towards unity. Perhaps the future will be more of a menace than a promise for the world. Liberation may degenerate into a series of isolated actions; the earth may once again become a wilderness, overwhelmed by excessive growth in consumption and exploitation. Perhaps utopian optimism should give place to critical pessimism? In philosophy, the influence of Ernst Bloch's 'principle of hope' is giving place to the 'negative dialectic' of Horkheimer and Adorno, to mention thinkers representing the two extremes of the Frankfurt school. All these influences have certainly played their part. Once more, as Henri Desroche has demonstrated so well,[27] a 'messianic' peak has been succeeded by a trough when hopes have been dashed. In their vague enthusiasm, political theologies without doubt confused a theological confession of the reality of the resurrection with the confirmation of this reality which might seem to have been provided by one brief stage of contemporary history, when hopes which have crumbled or been shattered were still high. Without question, a close succession of optimism and pessimism has played too large a part in the evolution of contemporary political theologies. Theology has reflected moods, rather than presenting proclamation and doctrine.

The singularity of the cross

At the same time, however, there has been an even more profound development. There has been a rediscovery of the identity of faith, of what René Marlé has called 'Christian singularity'.[28] The Bible as a whole is evidence that Judaeo-Christian faith is concerned with men's liberation, in the Old Testament with exodus from slavery and the journey towards the promised land of Canaan; in the New Testament with an earthly promise, the resurrection, the beginning of the new creation. The pernicious intrusion of spiritualism and individualism has masked this evidence. Political theologies do no more than develop a strain of messianic expectation, the first-fruits and pledges of which are seen by Christians in Jesus of Nazareth. That is why they have called him Christ, the Anointed One, the Messiah. However, unlike the liberations achieved through human agencies, whether these amount to a revolution in class relationships, an analysis of the workings of the unconscious, a new sense of cultural identity, or a restoration of social cohesion, this liberation brought about by the resurrection goes through the cross of Jesus Christ.

There is no question here of a great law of life, a claim that suffering brings maturity, an announcement of dawn at the dead of night. Such world-wide wisdom is as commonplace as it is improbable. No, the singularity of Christian faith lies in the way in which it associates liberation with two events which are neither commonplace nor assured: the death on the cross of a man in whom God reveals his fullness, and the reappearance of this man in whom God announces the raising of mankind now and at the last day. Is the word 'liberation' enough to express all this? Does it not tend to dissipate the uniqueness of faith in the futurism of hope, which is doomed to be frustrated by opposition? Would it not be better, as I suggested in an earlier chapter, to return to the classic term 'redemption',[29] with all that it implies about the imbalance between God's action and man's response, about God's independence and his intervention in man's favour at the very point when this man is himself thwarted? Be this as it may, it is the rediscovery of the uniqueness of Christianity which has led political theologies to meditate on the cross of Jesus Christ as the context of his resurrection and the way to it.

There is also a new consideration here of the two aspects, prospective and retrospective, of individual life and corporate history. Man is certainly characterized by openness, future promise, expectation, hope, but he also has roots, traditions, reflections, memories. As Freud has demonstrated so remarkably, man is always pulled in two directions. If he cannot be open, he becomes neurotic, but if he cannot contain himself, he explodes into delirium. A one-sided stress on the future is as lifeless as one-sided preoccupation with the past is deadly. An inability to accept the past is as much of a handicap as an inability to imagine the future. If hope has proved false, is this not to a large extent because it has been seen too much as a diversion, a way of forgetting, or as false modesty and blind desire? So it seems to me that political theologies have reverted to their meditations on the cross in order to retrieve the faculty of memory, in particular the memory of suffering inflicted and undergone, at a moment when history is no longer content with cherishing its hopes, but also remembers its distress. This development has been brought about by the temporal bipolarity of man and the world and a stress on the singularity of the risen Christ who had been crucified.

As with the resurrection, political theologies put forward interpretations of the cross which correspond to the cultural situation which they seek to address. They are not concerned with the cross apart from God, which so many modern thinkers have either celebrated in admiration or hated in disgust, with emotions ranging from romantic sorrow to humanist dignity. Nor are they concerned with the mystic cross through which

God and men share in the experience of sorrow. They are not even concerned with the expiatory cross, through which God takes upon himself, in the person of his Son, the death which ought to be the fate of sinful man, in order to give him divine life.

None of these interpretations, fruitful and powerful though they may be, satisfies contemporary political theology. They do not convey the true nature of God to men of today, with their eyes on the future and its hopes, yet at the same time haunted by the past and its sufferings. Like the theologies of hope and liberation, they too seek to involve God in change. The crucified God shares in the suffering of history, just as the risen God shares in its transformation. So for Moltmann, in particular, there is no contradiction between his first and second attempts; each time the central feature is the involvement of God in agony and in future developments. In *Theology of Hope*, the static God is replaced by the dynamic God, who accords those who follow him a share in this future of which he is the promise and not the termination. Similarly, in *The Crucified God*, the God who has been thought by classical theology to be impassible now becomes the suffering God, who involves those who follow him in his passion, so that they may in turn be able to share in the suffering of others. In theologies of resurrection, God moves from permanence to change. In theologies of the cross, God moves from impassibility to suffering. This is not the death of God, but there is no God without death, since God comes through death. Here the doctrine of the Trinity has an important role that it lacks in the theology of hope, which concentrates on a recognition of God's faithfulness to the promises by which he shows his future intentions to believers. By contrast, here the Trinity is the essential knowledge of God which is acquired by means of the cross. It is the union of the love of the Son, who gives his life, with the suffering of the Father, who abandons his Son to death, that gives rise to the Spirit, who opens up the future and brings life. The cross is the event which gives rise to a trinitarian understanding of God, because the trinitarian God is the crucified God.

The cross is the way to the inner knowledge of God, a knowledge which dismisses both theism and atheism. Neither of these views is capable of conceiving of God's personal involvement in human death; it is too much for atheism and too little for theism. That is why Moltmann always refuses to talk of redemption, substitution, vicarious expiation; he would obviously prefer to call it contagion through solidarity: 'By the secular cross on Golgotha, understood as open vulnerability and as the love of God for loveless and unloved, dehumanized man, God's being and God's life is open to true man.'[30] Here we have 'the event of suffering and liberating love'.

At this point, the earlier themes of liberation regain all their importance. There is, however, one difference. From now on, the remembrance of the cross makes it possible not only to look forward, towards the future, but also backward, towards the abyss, towards suffering, towards the vicious circles of individual and corporate existence from which God has now brought release. From now on, compassion is exercised with imagination. Political theologies address not only the entrepreneurs but those who back them up: not only those who work for change, but also those threatened with annihilation. The God who guides one group is the God who shows solidarity with the other.

Theology of Hope spoke above all of Christ inaugurating the future of the new world by his resurrection. *The Crucified God* speaks above all of Jesus in three roles: as the blasphemer, condemned by the law apart from its promise; as the rebel, suspected by the authorities who guess at the threat he poses; and as the one abandoned by God, who himself experiences suffering and death. Thus it is Jesus who demonstrates that God is truly a suffering God, if by suffering one means that God is capable of uniting within his person the contradiction between the death that he accepts and the life that he contains.

In that case there is considerable continuity between the two apparently opposed elements in political theology, even if it is rather strange that these two elements appear in reverse order. This contrast to the way in which they happened is without doubt the result of the reflections and reactions which I discussed earlier. First God opens up the future to hope; then he remembers suffering. Each time, the change in the image of God transforms man's understanding of himself and of the mission of the Christian community in the world. First of all, God disturbs and demolishes; then he suffers and sympathizes. These changes in God have political connotations, since they humanize man: first by hope and then by compassion. They are theologies, because they are concerned with God himself, and they are political, because they are concerned with the universal history of those who are affected by these changes. God's hope allows us to envisage the future not as an empty dream, a utopia, or in our own personal terms, but as a promise, a prolepsis, an anticipation, and certainly as a novelty. Furthermore, God's suffering allows us to see the past not so much as an overwhelming restraint, but rather as a companion to our progress. The continuity lies in the metamorphosis which God's presence brings about in both hope and human memory, in the militancy of action and the suffering of the passion. Consequently, in these two complementary books Moltmann believes that he has shown how God can be found both in necessary revolutions and in terrors undergone, in the Third World, or in Auschwitz. He is the trinitarian God who rises again at Easter and who dies on the cross. Thus God is involved in both the travail and the negativity of the world, relieving man of his unaided efforts both to liberate himself and to destroy himself.

The scope of this approach is impressive. In accordance with their original aim, political theologies have involved God in the changes of the world, trying not only to reflect these changes, but also to show the imminence of the resurrection and the cross of Jesus Christ.

Obscurities and questions

Theologies which are concerned to dissociate themselves from classical doctrines of redemption and the salvation of man by God, in order to stress the solidarity, the identification of God with man, do, however, leave several questions unanswered. They are interested not only in man's salvation, but also in the nature of God's self-revelation, as though the different understanding of God today meant that God had changed, as if a God from another age were confused with a God from elsewhere.

First of all, is not the trinitarian God so set about with human contradictions that he becomes a contradiction in himself? For example, if the Father himself dies and rises again, there is no conflict between the Son who dies, causing anguish to the Father, and the Father who raises the Son from the dead out of love for him. Failure to distinguish between the persons of the Trinity brings with it the risk of a Gnosticism in which a single divine nature undergoes a metamorphosis, in that its suffering is followed by resurrection, or rather insurrection. Such criticism might seem unfair, since Moltmann carefully rejects what the ancient church called the heresy of theopaschism or patripassianism,[31] that is to say the death of God. He keeps strictly to claiming that there is death in God. However, there is a constant ambivalence in his reflections, since the suffering of the Father who abandons the Son is constantly confused with the suffering of the Son who is abandoned. Is this just a piece of speculative subtlety? I doubt it, since it is of the essence of Christian faith to affirm the power of God at the very moment when he abandons the Son who offers himself; otherwise God's solidarity with mankind in his incarnation becomes God's confusion with mankind in its refusal of God. As well as being impossible in human terms, the resurrection then becomes even more unthinkable in theological terms. A form of redemption too external to mankind leads to identification without 'exteriorization' – to take up a term which is so dear to Moltmann. In this approach, by becoming man, God ceases to be God, and theology vacillates (as so often today) between the immanence of atheism and (in reaction) the transcendentalism of theism. We do not get a consistent picture of a living God by transforming him successively into a God who identifies himself with our hopes and then our sorrows. In his solidarity with man, God no longer remains God. His liberation (it can hardly be called redemption or salvation) becomes the impotence of fellow-suffering. God seems to be just one more man, so it is hard to see why he should still be called God. Yet God has the power to remain God the Creator, Saviour, Liberator, Recreator of man, at the very moment when he takes to himself human suffering and despair. God's passion does not sap his strength in any way. He has the power to humiliate himself for us, without annihilating himself with us. Otherwise his solidarity with us would get nowhere and his transformation would be a mysterious conjuring trick.

Furthermore, do we have to work with this dichotomy between the resurrection, which is bound up with man's active hope, and the cross, which is bound up with the memory of his sufferings? Is there not a deeper truth in the ancient descriptions which called the passion 'active', because it involves struggle and resistance, to the point of remaining defiantly silent, and the resurrection 'passive', because it involves astonished acceptance, to the point of the uneasy joy which goes with the acknowledgment of its reality? To live under the cross should be the characteristic of the fighting man, even in political life, where action is certainly not doomed to frustration, any more than Jesus was doomed to die. It is directed against adversity, without measuring truth by success or error by failure. To live by the resurrection should also be the characteristic of the fighting man, even in political life, where to go from one new start to another is doubtless the most realistic and truthful sign we have that hope does not need illusions to keep going. Thus it would be superficial to make too much of an amalgam of the cross, memory and sorrow, and resurrection, hope and optimism. One might be projecting human dispositions on to God instead of learning human strength from God. I feel that contemporary political theologies may have given way to such superficiality where they lack passiveness in the resurrection (it is better to put the problem like that, to keep the terminology within reasonable bounds), when they tone down the element

of surprise at the liberation it brings, and when they under-
estimate the 'activity', the force of the resistance that is
maintained in the cross.

Finally, there must certainly be a connection between
theology and politics. A theology which is not political is
limited to the mysteries of the soul. Human personality gains
nothing from such schizophrenia between religion as a private
affair, and politics as a secular, secularized, atheistic affair, for
all that an unhealthy alliance of bourgeois thought with
Marxist thought seeks to maintain it, with more or less culti-
vated indifference or police supervision. I also believe that any
theology which is not political lacks the assurance given by the
events of the cross and the resurrection, that it is in contact with
reality. Otherwise, at times it will see itself in terms of redemption, and the absoluteness of its claims will affect its programmes
and its pseudo-religious attempts at liberation, and at times its
lucidity will turn to cynicism and contempt. It is, in fact, the
absence of a theological and eschatological horizon or, to put
it more simply, the absence of resurrection in history and the
kingdom of God for history, which infects political life with the
taint of stratagem, self-interest and death. Thus even to
attempt a political theology is beneficial for both theology and
politics. Success is, however, hard to come by. Very often
politicians will regard the political theologies to which we have
devoted this chapter as purely theological works, without
analyses, theories or tactics. . . And sometimes theologians will
regard them as echoes of political arguments, seeking to make
their mark in theological discourse. Perhaps these two charges
are inevitable, since political theology is not concerned either
to present a Christian front or to indulge in political prophecy
on God's behalf. It depicts the involvement of God in earthly
history, in which his enterprise discloses him to be at work, and
characterizes history as a hope born of the cross. There is no
doubt, however, that we have to go beyond the present achievements of political theology, with its strength and its obscurity,
and to pursue our questions further. That is what I shall attempt
in the last chapter of this book: 'Spiritual Life and Politics'.

6

Spiritual Life and Politics

The problem of dualisms and the usefulness of distinctions

Dualisms usually run counter to experience, and consequently oblige thinkers to patch together what they have arbitrarily torn apart. Dualisms establish artificial divisions and lead to a hierarchy of values within which the spheres established by such divisions are classified. By way of example we might mention Platonic dualism, which distinguishes the world of the intellect above from the world of the senses below; or Cartesian dualism, which distinguishes thought without extension from extension without thought; or Marxist dualism, distinguishing economic infrastructures from political, cultural, moral and religious superstructures, which in the last resort are determined. In these three instances we can see a theory of knowledge deciding that there are two categories each with different natures, and a use of scholasticism to legitimate the theory. Each time, however, the course of intellectual history shows how the first cut of the scissors has severed a thread which later needs to be retied with scrupulous care. The holes which open up in the hull of the ship are constantly plugged until it founders for good and another dualism floats to the surface of the changing waters.

A classic dilemma: the temporal and the spiritual

The same thing seems to happen when we try to separate spiritual life from politics. We might begin with Jesus' famous reply to the Pharisees, who were more friends of God than

friends of Caesar. On this occasion they were allied with the
Herodians, who were more friends of Caesar than of God. They
came together to lay a dualistic trap: ' "Is it lawful to pay taxes
to Caesar, or not?" But Jesus, aware of their malice, said,
"Why put me to the test, you hypocrites? Show me the money
for the tax." And they brought him a coin. And Jesus said to
them, "Whose likeness and inscription is this?" They said,
"Caesar's." Then he said to them, "Render therefore to
Caesar the things that are Caesar's, and to God the things that
are God's" ' (Matt. 22.17–21).

The strange thing is that Jesus is often supposed to have
fallen into the trap laid for him. This passage, which in the
context of the gospels serves as a hortatory parable, uses an
actual situation (with a good deal of hypocritical distortion) as
the basis of an appeal for a costly obedience towards God
(which is carefully omitted). Since Jesus tells both sides that
they are already Caesar's subjects, and he now urges them to
become God's servants, his reply has been understood to
establish the basic charter of the separation between the
spiritual and the temporal, the internal and the external, the
eternal and the transitory, between God and Caesar.

A great many analyses have been concerned to make these
distinctions more precise. The temporal is transitory. It is
human and relative. It comprises whatever passes and fades
away; we should not become too involved in it nor should we
expect too much from it. It is also tainted. It requires compro-
mise with violence, in conquest or oppression. It transforms the
victims of today into the executioners of tomorrow. It deforms
those who set out to reform society. Maurice Barrès unmasks it
from the right wing: 'Political man is a tight-rope walker. He
keeps his balance by saying the opposite of what he does.'
Roger Martin du Gard chastises it from the left: 'To have a
political sense is to accept the use in the social conflict of
procedures which any of us would reject in private disputes as
being dishonest and criminal.' By contrast, the spiritual is
eternal. It is divine and absolute. It requires our total dedica-
tion, because here our ultimate destiny is at stake. The spiritual

rejects means which are inadequate for its ends. It avoids covetousness and defensiveness. Forsaking human society, it seeks the city on high of which God is the sole architect. That is why we tend to contrast mysticism and politics, the saint and the commissar, St Francis of Assisi and Machiavelli, to single out the classic instances.

I may have caricatured this dualism, but in any case it is a thousand times more disquieting than it is reassuring. In contrast to the incarnation, it separates God's spirit from man's politics. It leads to detachment and opposition, where faith looks for obedience and permeation. It reduces spiritual life to the level of spiritualism and it confines political life to materialistic scorn. Spiritual life becomes evanescent, a heavenly cloud on the horizon of the earth and of history. Faith is a balloon ascent, with a number of parachute drops. Above all, it is so like an optional extra to the hard slog of life that we constantly find ourselves asking where people (others and ourselves) could have found it, hidden it or lost it. It is easy to go on from there, as Jean Guéhenno once did, to argue that believers are ambushed by heaven. As for political life, it takes precautions against this spiritual life as though it were a germ. Some argue that the spiritual life infinitely surpasses politics (in which case, why go on bothering with political theology, if contemplative life or existence by faith or the transcendent revelation of God constitute the sole supreme good?), while others believe it to contain an irreducible relic of idealism (in that case, however, why go on calling oneself a Christian, taking one's bearings by Jesus of Nazareth, reading the Bible and meeting together, rather than quite simply allowing these spiritual remnants to be swallowed up in the world of politics?). In both cases, we remain with a complete dualism. The trinitarian God: the Father and Creator, the Son and Reconciler, the Spirit and Lifegiver, does not enter human politics. And human history does not involve a calling, is not lived out from a cross and resurrection, and does not progress towards a kingdom. We put asunder what God has joined together, and that is without doubt the clearest definition of sin.

A no less ambiguous modern dualism: idealism and materialism

Today this dualism is expressed most clearly in the opposition between idealism and materialism. Unfortunately, these terms are always used to characterize Christianity on the one hand and Marxism on the other; this makes any debate between the two on fundamental issues impossible, because the labels on the goods are deceptive. According to the Bible, there is nothing idealistic about God in the sense that materialist theorists attribute to the term. For them, idealism affirms the priority of the conscience or of thought over matter or over nature in the development of the universe and in the explanation of social phenomena. To maintain such an interpretation would be to transform the living God, the Word who challenges mankind, into a primordial idea or a spiritual energy. However, the Word is not an idea, nor is the Logos incarnate in Jesus the Logos of the idealist philosophers. Otherwise, it would be too easy to see the Logos as an element in metaphysical spiritualism, which would automatically exclude it from historical materialism. It would be deliberately to ignore the way in which God is shown to work in the Bible. Here the important thing is not the primitive character of the anthropomorphisms, but the aptness of the terms which are applied to him: God is totally invisible to the unbeliever, totally present to the believer, as though he had a body with face, ears, hands, heart and entrails.

Biblical language about God is metaphorical and corporate. These two terms are meant to mark it off from any approach which seeks to reduce God to a supreme idea, infinite and absolute. In fact, we need constantly to invent a language which distinguishes God both from the transcendence of the idea and the immanence of matter, since these are the two tombs, the one speculative and the other evolutionary, to which people have come to bury his corpse. Likewise, God is not to be found beyond history, but through it. He is neither its solemn complement nor its spiritual atmosphere, but the one who intervenes in it personally. That is why in this book I have done my best to distinguish him both from the ancient realm of eternal meta-

physical ideas and from the new realm of meta-historical
utopian ideas, and I have tried to keep to the notion of meta-
textual concomitance, which signifies the presence of God here
and now: towards man, for man and with man.

If we need one last token of the impropriety of combining
faith with idealism, we can find it in the biblical miracles. In
the Bible, miracles are never miraculous in the modern sense,
performed to further beliefs and contrary to scientific laws.
They are wonders, aimed at showing that God's mercy affects
men's bodies as well as their souls and that his glory is witnessed
to by the homage of flesh as well as spirit. We know that when
speaking of man the Bible calls him either flesh or spirit, body
or soul, since it is from the heart (and not only from the body)
that mistrust and failure proceed, and it is in the body (and
not only in the soul) that God's renewal makes itself known.
There could hardly be a more unsuitable or mistaken word to
qualify (or in Marxist eyes to disqualify) biblical faith than
idealism.

Similarly, however, the choice of the word materialism (even
though this is dialectical and not mechanistic) always seems to
me to involve Marxism in scholastic embarrassments which
could have been avoided had Marx judiciously kept to his first
choice of vocabulary in the manuscripts of 1844. In contrast to
Hegel, who gave a speculative explanation of universal history
in terms of the phenomenology of the absolute Spirit, Marx put
forward his own historical and genetic explanation, based on
the importance of social relationships in natural development.
At this point, the distinction drawn by Marx was not between
spiritualism and materialism, but between spiritualism and
naturalism, which is neither the idealism of culture nor the
materialism of production. To quote him: 'Whenever real,
corporeal man, man with his feet firmly on the solid ground,
man exhaling and inhaling all the forces of nature. . . When he
creates, he only posits objects, because he is posited by objects
– because at bottom he is nature. . . Here we see how consistent
naturalism or humanism is distinct from both idealism and
materialism, and constitutes at the same time the unifying truth

of both. We see how subjectivity and objectivity, spirituality and materiality, activity and suffering, lose their antithetical character, and thus their existence as such antitheses only within the framework of society.'³²

In the first stage of Marxist vocabulary, there is still no block between explanatory truth and the materialism of the means of production. So there can still be useful discussion of the eternal question at issue between faith and agnosticism: is nature all that there is, finding its destination in its evolution, or is there a God who is the Word for mankind, a God who does not violate the laws of nature by supernatural additions or interventions, but transforms nature into creation, in so far as the natural man is given a vocation, a promise and a commandment in history, which is addressed to him by his creator? Understood in this way, the dialogue between believers and Marxists can continue to be a useful discussion for both sides about the reality of nature and the possibility of a revelation in history. There is no confusing conflict between two opposed metaphysical systems: materialism, for which Marxism claims to have scientific evidence, and idealism, which Marxists believe to be characteristic of all religions, including Christianity, and against which they put forward their assertion of the progress of human knowledge.

Unfortunately, Marx became polemical and preferred the word materialism to naturalism in his subsequent writings. His explanation became metaphysical, and he had to try to fit scientific and historical facts to it. As I said earlier, this tied him to an unexamined dualistic presupposition on the basis of which he sought to prove that in all times and in all places economic infrastructures (i.e. matter in the sciences and the masses in history) have a determining effect on cultural superstructures (i.e. conscience and ideology). This seems to me to have turned Marxism into an inverse form of Hegelianism, which is just as metaphysical and speculative. Compared with Christianity, Marxism has given rise to a serious and basic misunderstanding, because it has turned the fundamental debate over the autonomy of nature and the significance of revelation, the debate between agnosticism and faith, into a speculative dispute about the conflict between materialism and idealism. The Marx of 1844 was aware of this false dichotomy. Thus the dialogue between believers and Marxists which is so useful and necessary has been burdened by an irresolvable quarrel between two metaphysical interpretations, as though biblical faith were tied to an idealistic vision and Marxist analysis to a materialistic theory. So it seems to me that the first differentiations need to be made on this theoretical level. Once this misunderstanding has been recognized, combated and overcome, it will be possible for a lasting and really free debate to begin, since the freedom to believe implies the freedom to be an atheist, and the freedom to be an atheist implies the freedom to believe.

So far I have tried to combat the unfortunate consequences of dualism. I would not want the title of this last chapter, 'Spiritual Life and Politics', to lead to a divorce between the two and a hierarchy of values, with one superior to the other, depending on whether one heeds the appeal to spiritual detachment from the emptiness of politics or prefers Feuerbach's exhortations: 'Instead of being friends of God, we must become friends of man; instead of being believers, we must become thinkers; instead of being beggars, we must become workers; instead of being candidates for the beyond, we must become students of this world.' I believe that dualism separates man from God and God from man. It is a structure which leads to detachment, whereas the Bible leads to alliance. It is a schizophrenic attitude, whereas the Bible calls for reconciliation. It is the misfortune of being solitary, when benefits derive from communication.

Two useful distinctions

We must now tackle the other part of the title, the attempt to draw real distinctions between spiritual life and politics. I can see two. Spiritual life, that is to say life lived under the Spirit of the living God, does not provide political solutions. These arise out of analyses of particular situations. The Bible has such a specific setting that it does not contain programmes which are capable of adaptation. Any direct move from the spiritual realm to politics ends up either in the hallowing of a particular regime (or a revolution), the source of which lies elsewhere, or in an investment in politics of an expectation which should be met elsewhere. State order becomes providence and revolution becomes redemption. Caesar plays at Christ and Christ plays at anti-Caesar. This can produce Antigone, inevitably condemned by the power of Creon. It bears no resemblance to Jesus. Jesus does not ask Pilate to crucify him in order to fulfil the inevitable destiny of the powerful, which is always evil, but to deliver him by the political administration of justice. Similarly, the prophets did not ask the kings to cease to be kings, but to exercise their kingship in accordance with justice. Life according to the spirit is not therefore a magical short-circuit to political work. No magic is involved in the inspiration of the gospels. They are, rather, a challenge to believers to steep themselves in the complexities of history.

In this respect we can understand the disconcerting effect on Marx of the 'spiritual' disinterest in politics of those who sought to replace the troublesome business of making analyses by the intoxication of sentiment. 'Kriege sets out for war in order to take seriously the desires of the heart. However, this is not the real, profane heart, filled with bitterness at the reality of misery, a heart swelled by sweet and happy dreams. At the same time, he gives evidence of a "religious heart" by entering the struggle as a priest under another name, as a representative of the poor. . . Here there is a sublime sentiment which, in hours of solitude and discouragement, swells the heart of a brave man and compensates him for all the vexations of this evil world.'[33] 'The phrase which corresponded to this imagined liquidation of class relations was *fraternité*, universal fraternization and brotherhood. This pleasant abstraction from class antagonisms, this sentimental equalization of contradictory class interests, this fantastic elevation above the class struggle, *fraternité*, this was really the special catch-cry of the February revolution.'[34]

Thus spiritual life is dangerous both as an elixir of enthusiasm and as an opium of resignation. That is why, in the New Testament, Jesus does not advise political men to imitate the noble folly of spiritual men. The 'sons of the light' are, rather, to learn from the thoughtfulness, the prudence, the tenacity of the 'sons of this world'. 'The sons of this world are wiser in their own generation than the sons of light' (Luke 16.8). Or again, 'For which of you, desiring to build a tower, does not first sit down and count the cost, whether he has enough to complete it?' (Luke 14.28), which is a strange preface to the spiritual conclusion which follows: 'So therefore, whoever of you does not renounce all that he has cannot be my disciple' (Luke 14.33)!

So if there is a real distinction between spiritual life and political life, it is not that the former should overwhelm the latter with its unconsidered generosity, but on the contrary that the spiritual man in each of us should learn from the politician, from his calculated tactics, from his long-term planning, from his concern about the forces at his disposal, and from his skill at taking advantage of opportunities, good or bad. Political life is a parable for spiritual life, because it cannot escape into promises and complaints. It has both to theorize and to act. So it ballasts the spiritual life with intelligence and perforce with modesty. It keeps it from idle religious or moralistic chatter, from desires or condemnations which do not involve calculation or implementation. So this first distinction is contrary to what is usually thought of as spiritual purity (as opposed to political impurity). The Bible always turns things upside down by suggesting that the church, with its words, should learn from the world, with its reflections and actions.

There is also, however, a second distinction. It does not do away with the first, but adds a touch of radicalism without which life according to the Spirit is reduced to a lifeless spiritualism. To begin with, let us go to the heart of God's extraordinary nature and the real character of his theological perfection: 'Love your enemies and pray for those who persecute you, so that you may be sons of your Father who is in heaven; for he makes his sun rise on the evil and on the good, and sends rain on the just and on the unjust. . . You, therefore, must be perfect, as your heavenly Father is perfect' (Matt. 5.44f., 48). As far as politics goes, these seem to be the most impracticable words in the whole Bible. However, I would see them as the most spiritual of comments on political life, if politics is not content with being retributive and vindictive, corporalist and nationalist, and seeks to be a source of renewal, solidarity and international brotherhood. This is the spiritual choice facing all politics. We have already noted that the calculation and caution necessary in politics made it a parable of the nature of spiritual life. Are we to say that such an end excludes such means, or that such necessary means exclude such an impossible end? We might say, rather, that at this point spiritual life ceases to be an optional extra for political life and becomes a problematical yet necessary motive power. Any political regime, no matter what its democratic legitimacy or its revolutionary origin may be, which has stopped trying to use its power in the service of those who, in terms of the gospel, seem to be (or even are) wicked and injust, is doomed to lose its soul, even if it has conquered the world. In practice, however, politicians tend to leave out this spiritual requirement, which is why it is necessary to continue to distinguish between political and spiritual life.

I have deliberately chosen to avoid the problem of church-state relationships, but the tension certainly needs to be pointed out. However, historically it is far too complicated by actual power struggles. I have also rejected the Lutheran division between the spiritual power of forgiveness in the church and the temporal power of the law in the state.[35] This distinction may avoid the ancient confusions of clerical spiritualism and the newer ones of temporal redemption, but it also risks removing tension from political life and robbing it of any spiritual dimensions. It is the end of peace with one's enemies, a chance for the 'wicked', reintegration for the 'unjust', in short, power to restore everyone to a place in life rather than giving them simply what is their due. An animal is not political, in the way in which it is essentially territorial and instinctual. If man is a political animal, he has this character to the degree to which he can share with, and enter into, contracts with others. That is why he always tries, as far as possible within any given limits, to pursue the process of becoming human and (in spite of what Marx says about his idealistic errors) to strive for political brotherhood at the heart of a fratriarchy in conflict.

Two great models of society as candidates for baptism

In all political societies, men institute certain legal rules which either correspond with biological instincts or take their place when they disappear. This happens, for example, in the sphere of sexuality and parenthood, of property and power, and of religion and culture. These rules are the framework of political society. They are meant to give it a certain stability. By agreeing with them and yielding to them, members of political societies both profit from them and suffer under them. They receive their due and they qualify for both duties and benefits. Politics cannot exist without such rules, which naturally vary depending on the disposition of forces, ideological schematizations and historical projects. So there is a constant interaction between biology and law, between power and rules, between evolution and stability. Politics must always take account of these two factors, since without power law is quickly ridiculed, but without law the interplay of forces makes society impossible or, more probably, leads to the return of animal societies, within which there is a constant struggle for recognition at a time when biological domination is recognized, contested, re-established or provided with a substitute. So while there may be animal societies, strictly speaking there is no such thing as a political animal, because with animals hostile confrontations and the dominance of instincts take the place of contracts and juridical rules in human societies.[36]

Political rules are meant to guarantee relatively stable

coexistence between members of society. Revolutions do not
contradict this general aim, since they always seek a stability
which will be an improvement on what has gone before
because it is more firmly based on justice. In this respect,
revolutions too work towards the establishment of order, unless
they are content to destroy with no thought for reconstruction.
The fact that they can end in disintegration or terror only
emphasizes the faults of the political order against which they
are directed. Besides, an examination of the reasons for the
failure of revolutions has always been the greatest spur to
political reflection. For example, Hegel believed that the
French Revolution ultimately failed because of a constitution
which was incapable of safeguarding the liberty of its citizens,
whereas Marx believed that the popular revolution was
gradually taken over by the middle classes. We can easily find
parallels to these two different approaches in contemporary
assessments of the future prospects of the Soviet, Chinese or
Cuban revolutionaries. The important thing, then, is that a
certain order should be established, and that revolutions are
the midwives to this new birth.

Biblical faith gives no detailed indication of the nature of this
political order. We see it change with the social organization of
Israel: a tribal confederation; temporary, charismatic judges
who do not found a dynasty; a hereditary monarchy and the
fragmentation of the kingdom; deportation; colonial dependence; wars of independence; controlled independence; and
then a last revolt leading to annihilation. One might say that
every kind of political regime is attempted and often endured
without the establishment of any lasting ideal. In fact, the
political theologies elaborated over the history of the church
have modelled themselves more on secular thought than on
biblical history. For example, one popular occupation was to
compare the advantages and disadvantages of the four regimes
distinguished and made into a hierarchy by Plato, in accordance
with a pattern of historical degeneration: timocracy, where
power is wielded by the worthiest, though here the military
already often get the better of the philosophers; oligarchy,

where privilege becomes the monopoly of the richest; democratic reaction against oligarchy, which unfortunately leads to anarchy; and then of course tyranny, the rule of an individual, which is the final outcome of this internal dissolution.

There is little argument in contemporary political theology about the best form of constitutional government, because economic models obviously have so much influence on models of the state. Here, too, however, biblical faith does not give us an ideal model or a durable one. The models are taken from neighbouring societies. Believers have to decide whether they are willing or able to baptize them. Baptizing a structure and not a person is always a dubious business. Theologically, at any rate, a person asks of his or her own free will to be incorporated into this great movement that affords a link with the cross, conversion, resurrection and renewal, all of which come from Jesus Christ. This sort of thing does not happen with a social structure. The believing community has to adapt and adjust to the social community, taking over an existing economic practice and an ideology drawn from elsewhere, which it must criticize, correct, improve and (if necessary) change, knowing full well that they are alien. However, I have extended the application of the image of baptism to social structures and political regimes as well, because it has three features which help us to define the situation. Social structures already exist before their baptism and by nature they are pagan. At the time of their baptism, these structures will prove to have various failings. After their baptism, they should call for renewal. Will the water be deep enough to wash away inner corruption? Will it have sufficient cleansing power to put a new complexion on the society which lives according to a particular social model?

As far as I can see, the church has tried to baptize two great social models. First, there is that of the common good. This does not derive from the Bible but from the ancient city-state: it belongs to what I have elsewhere called the metaphysical period. The other is the classless society. This is not a biblical model, either, but stems from Marxist revolutions: it corresponds

to what I have called the meta-historical period. I now propose to put each of them through a brief baptismal catechism
or, if that seems rather pretentious, to assess their prophetic
openness or their critical usefulness. At any event, these two
models offer the best opportunity for a spiritual contribution
since, as we have already remarked so often, there is no rational
possibility of elaborating a biblical pattern of economics,
much less a biblical pattern of politics.

The common good and necessary hierarchies

The common good would seem to have many similarities to a
biblical social ethic. Does it not attach prime importance to
interpersonal solidarity, rejecting both egocentric individualism
and the anonymity of the state? Does it not seek to understand
all society in terms of the nuclear family, where human relationships are felt most strongly, and the body of the church, where
spiritual relationships are lived out to the full? Does it not
affirm with the wisdom of reason and the ardour of faith that
we need one another, that we form a single people, and that it
is therefore necessary to break down opposition when it tends
to provoke division? The common good is an optimistic and
demanding model. It is based on the principle that a given
society has an agreed objective, the realization of which calls
for unquestioning obedience.

However, the common good remains a model which has not
taken very well to baptism. At all times it has tended to give its
blessing to the continuation of hierarchies which are supposed
to be necessary for the good of society. Historically speaking,
the common good has always been the opposite to having
goods in common. If the group is to function, everyone has to
remain in the place he has by virtue of his birth, possessions or
ability. It is worth introducing a number of quotations:
'Ideally conceived, society is an organism of different grades,
and human activities form a hierarchy of functions, which
differ in kind and significance, but each of which is of value on
its own plane, provided that it is governed, however remotely,

by the end which is common to all. Like the celestial order, of
which it is the dim reflection, society is stable, because it is
straining upwards. . . Each member has its own function,
prayer, or defence, or merchandise, or tilling the soil. Each
must receive the means suited to its station, and must claim no
more. Within classes there must be equality . . . between classes
there must be inequality.'[37]

Or, in the Pope's own words: 'It is impossible to reduce
human society to a level. The *Socialists* may do their worst, but
all striving against nature is vain. There naturally exist among
mankind innumerable differences of the most important kind;
people differ in capability, in diligence, in health, and in
strength; and unequal fortune is a necessary result of inequality
of condition. Such inequality is far from being disadvantageous
either to individuals or to the community; social and public
life can only go on by the help of various kinds of capacity and
the playing of many parts, and each man, as a rule, chooses the
part which peculiarly suits his case. . . If any there are who
pretend differently – who hold out to a hard-pressed people
freedom from pain and trouble, undisturbed repose, and
constant enjoyment – they cheat the people and impose upon
them, and their lying promises will only make the evil worse
than before. There is nothing more useful than to look at the
world as it really is – and at the same time to look elsewhere
for a remedy to its troubles.'[38]

Besides, it depends on the generosity of the rich, the patience
of the poor, the progressive acquisition of private property by
the largest possible number, saving them from being exploited
and remaining dependent on the state, and finally on the
recognition of God's special concern for the unfortunate and
the gift of his grace in all circumstances to both rich or poor.
In short, the common good is an indigestible mixture of
courageous and profound spiritual truths with a reverent
resignation over natural and social inequalities. The astonishing
thing is that it is actually called the common good, when in
fact it is the inevitable and in some respects beneficial result of
a hierarchical diversity of conditions. Hence the obvious

question: has the common good ever been anything but a spiritualizing commendation of different situations in terms of their loftiest aims: a stable society in this world and retribution in the world to come? In any case, discussion of the common good has always been carried on by those with a favourable position in society, since it offers a justification for the privileges of the conservatives, who benefit even when their views are sincerely held.

To be sure, the texts which I have quoted come from ancient times and are in line with particular ideological convictions: feudal hierarchies in the Middle Ages and bourgeois paternalism in the nineteenth century. The facts are very different in contemporary society. De Tocqueville was right and Marx wrong in their expectations, since in place of the growing impoverishment of the masses and a monopoly bringing wealth to a decreasing minority, we have seen the rise of the middle classes. As Valéry Giscard d'Estaing puts it: 'Far from leading to a sharp and hostile confrontation between the middle classes and the proletariat, present developments have led to the expansion of a vast and somewhat amorphous central group which is called on to provide a context for the integration of French society as a whole. It can fulfil this role, progressively and peacefully, by virtue of its rapid numerical growth, its affinity with other categories of society, its open character and the modern values which it communicates.'[39]

While the positive features of this description are to be welcomed, in the end its geographical application is very limited. People nowadays do not dare to talk about the common good, because that model is out of fashion. But would it not be a more realistic paradigm today than in ancient times, when people used it constantly to disguise the inexorable reality of a hierarchical society? Conversely, the other model which we shall go on to consider, that of the class struggle, harbinger of a classless society, has become fashionable at the very point when it is least appropriate as a paradigm for the present stage of social development. Be this as it may, there are many signs that the common good is often in process of becoming a necessary model: the progressive impoverishment of the masses in industrial society, social contracts in the public sector, the narrowing of the spread in salaries as societies develop, the homogenization of culture, the alternation in power of parties concerned to retain their middle-of-the-road support, and perhaps above all the joint management of crises when these are really formidable.

Having said this, however, there are some things about which we should be clear. This new common good is a virtue born of necessity and not a natural or providential ideal. The workers had to fight for their stake in the economy. The new common good has come about through a reduction of inequalities, not through an attempt to use them as incitements. Those with privileges do not collaborate; they yield. Hierarchies do not perpetuate themselves; they co-operate under pressure. As a result, far from being a natural datum, the common good can prove to be a gradual, or even a violent, conquest. The common good is not the antithesis of class struggle. Sometimes it can lead to it. It should be noted that developments as it were within industrial societies are not paralleled at a global level. Here the disparities are greater than ever before in the course of human history, simply because there is often no way, no desire to fight against an oppressive domination, against overwhelming odds.

If, then, we try to baptize the common good, as the Christian church did in ancient times, we must not seem to give a seal of approval to the *status quo*. We must plunge this natural child, this bastard of the ancient city-state and the Christian republic, into the deep waters of conversion. In short, the common good must be seen as the possible outcome of conflicts but not as the prohibition of these conflicts on the pretext that inequality is natural. It is a necessary stimulus to society, hallowed by the wisdom of divine providence.

The class struggle and the classless society

Should we then change the candidate for baptism and, having blessed the common good, go on to bless the classless society as the future outcome of total involvement in the present class struggle? This second model might also seem to have many similarities to a biblical social ethic. It puts forward a brotherly kingdom in terms of struggles for liberation. It sees history in terms of oppressions which have been banished, alienations which have disappeared, separations which have been overcome, and corporate guilt which is in process of elimination. Its optimism is bound up with the hope of a meta-historical future, whereas the optimism engendered by the common good was bound up with the harmony of the metaphysical present. To highlight these contrasts is not to practise the worst kind of politics but to unmask hidden privileges in order to abolish. The class struggle is not against people, but against the structures which separate people. It is therefore a mistake to condemn the class struggle for having a taste for destruction and violence, when politically it expresses a thirst for a new brotherhood and the development of a creative community. One quotation should be enough: 'The classless society will be a fully developed expression of man's domination over natural forces, both over nature which is properly so called and over human nature. It will be the fulfilment of all his creative capacities, in other words, a development of all human powers in their own right, without being measured by a pre-established standard.'[40] We can understand how the prophetic, messianic and apocalyptic atmosphere of the Bible can reappear in such aspirations and how Christians today can turn from the static ideal of the common good towards the dynamism of the classless society. Or, to put it another way, just as there has long been an alliance between faith and order, there is now a new one between hope and revolution.

However, I must also raise the question I asked of the common good: can this model be baptized in waters deep enough to cleanse and purify it? Here, too, we have a natural child, a bastard born of modern revolutions and Christian brotherhood. The one who does not baptize is content to legitimate. He becomes a disciple instead of a prophet. He hallows instead of feeling free to attack, which is the only guarantee of being able to feel equally free to defend.

Let me ask three questions about the classless society. They might be regarded as part of a baptismal catechism, without forgetting in the least that the world is not really a candidate for baptism. What we are trying to do is to find a place for Christian faith in the modern world of the class struggle, just as the church once tried to find a place in the ancient, harmonious world of the common good. Granted, there is a great deal of difference between the two situations: the common good was baptized into Christianity when ancient society had collapsed and the Christian community had to compensate for the failure of civil society. By contrast, the class struggle is a post-Christian affair, in a period when modern society is becoming emancipated from ecclesiastical tutelage. However, such distinctions are only relative. At the time of an attempt at baptism (or acculturation), the candidate is always recalcitrant and there are always some good questions which can be asked before the certificate is handed out. And of course he will use this to justify his existing nature, rather than as a way of transforming himself in accordance with the faith.

My first question concerns the degree of non-scientific utopia contained in the expectation of the classless society. If the common good is an idealistic illusion about the present, is not the classless society an idealistic illusion about the future? Idealism simply takes a different form in each case: at one time in metaphysics, and now in utopia. Each time, however, the characteristics are the same: virtue and judgment, promise and deceit. For the threat to social theory is always posed by idealism and never by materialism. This happens even with Marxism. All the socialist societies (to each according to his work) recognize that they have not yet reached the stage of being communist societies (to each according to his needs). However, is this 'not yet' an explicable delay or an indefinite

postponement? The choice here in fact depends on the degree
of secular faith to be retained in the infallibility of a theory
which is incapable of historical verification. We should remember the successive misadventures of Marxism, the seizing of
power by minorities, undemocratic centralization and personality cults, none of which can be explained theoretically in
terms of the economic infrastructure which remains socialistic.
Then there are conflicts and schisms between the socialist
countries, and a pluralism of models depending on possible
combinations and their attraction to the electorate, and so on.
In a word, we have seen a fallible history and not the infallible
predictions of a theory.

Christians can assert all this in a brotherly way, because there
seems to be a strange affinity (I would not go so far as to say a
systematic parallel) between the historic destiny of the Christian
community and that of the Marxist community. To begin with,
we might point to two fundamental experiences which came to
grief at the start and later became ideals: the Jerusalem
community and the Paris commune. Then there have been
long periods of a dogmatic constitution combined with persecutions by outsiders: from St Paul to Constantine, from Karl Marx
to Lenin. Then came opportunities and the real test, gaining
power: Constantine and Charlemagne, Lenin and Stalin.
There have also been schisms, which have not automatically
been either heresies or deviations: Rome and Constantinople,
Moscow and Peking, Luther and Tito. Today there is a
World Council of Churches but not yet a World Council of
Marxists. That should be enough of these fraternal ironies of
history. They give the lie to infallibility without necessarily
leading to scepticism, if it is true that hope begins only when we
have lost our illusions. But Marxism needs to be based on a
permanent theory of the cross, and not just a transitory theory
of alienation. It remains the fact that the classless society must
cease to be a future heavenly compensation for present earthly
difficulties. Meta-history has been too ready to dress up the
future in the attributes of classical metaphysics: universality,
perpetuity, absoluteness. Here even Gramsci proves to be a

metaphysician and a theologian in disguise: 'Marxism provides an infallible method, an instrument of great precision for exploring the future and predicting corporate developments in order to guide and thus master them.'[41]

The second question is: is the classless society, which is an ideal of social brotherhood, equally an ideal for political government? In fact, according to Marxist theory, political parties are only ideological superstructures, expressing and disguising the real conflict of economic interests. So it is logical and by no means totalitarian that multiple political parties should disappear when the classless society is achieved, with the minor addition of an involvement of non-party members in the life of the state. Now we can see how in the practice of socialist countries the absence of a plurality of political parties makes social criticism impossible; it soon becomes civil treason. It gives rise to a constant temptation towards personal or corporate totalitarianism. So it is by no means certain that the classless society is an ideal in this respect; perhaps it is an ideological weight hung round the necks of socialist states, and of communists who do not live in socialist countries. From now on they have to produce their evidence: they have to bring about the coexistence of collective Marxist liberation with all the political, cultural, religious and personal liberties which socialist societies reject. Still, while I have no doubt about the sincerity of the practical concern I have described, I have to ask myself what theoretical foundation can be discovered for the realization of the utopia of the classless society. It is hard to see how the theory of the unity of the proletariat can provide a basis for the permanent existence of multiple political parties. At the least, it is necessary to deny emphatically that politics is determined by economic infrastructures.

Until a theoretical revision is made at this fundamental level, we shall always have to tread the tightrope between the fragility of goodwill and tactical opportunism. This is a matter of abandoning the dualism that I mentioned earlier. The dualistic approach argues that economic infrastructures always dominate political, cultural and religious superstructures. Does not the hard core of Marxism, its dogma, lie here, rather than in materialism, dialectic or atheism? To ask Marxism to give that up is surely to kill it rather than to baptize it. Let the statement remain in the form of a question, but it is a fundamental one. At this point the Marxists can see it as clearly as the non-Marxists. I do, however, have the feeling that they still prefer tactical accommodation to a baptismal transformation and that they do not know how to introduce a permanent multi-party system, which is a necessity in the economic theory of the class struggle, as a prelude to a classless society. Then there will be a single party.

And now the final question. The class struggle tends to use too simple a Manichaean type of explanation to tackle the presence of evil and its resurgence at the heart of human liberty. By externalizing evil and projecting it on to the scape-goats of capitalism and imperialism, it can never see itself clearly. It is doomed to either blindness or deception. Conflict will be necessary, as I think I have established, because the common good is never a natural datum, nor a harmonious hierarchy, but a battle over privileges, a fight against hier-archies. With only two classes, however, especially when they have to separate into two distinct camps, there is always a risk that the fundamental antagonism between the good (on our side) and the bad (on the other side) will be reconstructed in social terms. In that case there is a relapse into moralism and metaphysics, even if in other respects the question is one of available forces and tactics. Idealism is reconstructed under the guise of ideology, and as in all idealism, the obvious distance between theory and practice has a demoralizing effect. The oppressors all belong to the opposite camp. As for one's own camp, by virtue of its virgin birth and immaculate protection it always becomes the vehicle of concrete universality and justice incarnate. The masses are an infallible source of inspiration and their leaders are infallible interpreters. 'If history's attitude to truth depends on the opinion of the mass, the opinion of the mass is absolute, infallible, it is law for history. In that case it is the mass which assigns history its task and its activity.'[42] Could a prophet, an apostle or a biblical apocalyptic writer, in their solitude, talk like this? Has not the twentieth century tended to proliferate ideological ostracism in the same way that the nineteenth century proliferated private ostracism? Have we not simply shifted the contexts of Pharisaism, the Inquisition and excommunication, to use words the religious connotations of which are well known? The class struggle has a necessary element of conflict, whereas the common good tended to ignore it by hallowing hierarchical differences. But the class struggle risks promising more than it can deliver. It risks suppressing control by a plurality of political parties once it issues in a classless society. And in the end it risks shifting Manichaean moralism from private to public life.

Fratriarchal conflict, a more realistic and promising social model

I have no intention of dismissing two real social models in order to propose a third, which is obviously better because it is purely imaginary. In fact, I myself feel that at a global level, the model of the class struggle is much more relevant today than that of the common good, because of the disparities which so threaten the world in this last quarter of the twentieth century. That is true even if there is some chance of achieving the model of the common good in those rare societies, like our own, which are both privileged and under threat. However, my concern has not been to deduce one or other model from the Bible. Neither of them is biblical in any way. For both of them, however, baptism, criticism and transformation would be beneficial. As we have seen, the bibilical model is that of conflict in the fratriarchy. It has more conflict to it than the common good, with its fear of disputes and its dissimulation of hierarchies. The model is, however, a fratriarchy, and this is not the case with the class struggle, combining as it does a dualistic moralism in the present and an uncontrolled idealism in the future. According to the Bible, brothers do not have a common good, nor are their interests complementary. They struggle constantly with temptations towards jealousy, injustice and stratagem. However, not one of them is appointed judge, exterminator or examiner of his other brethren. In the course of history, their fratriarchy is constantly disrupted and reconstituted, with the biblical promise and the biblical reality that the cross in the past will bring resurrection in the future.

I have a feeling that conflict within the fratriarchy is a more realistic social model (more materialistic, if one likes to put it that way) than the idealism of the common good in the present or the idealism of the classless society in the future. That is why I have argued that meta-textual existence with the texts which describe the disruptions and the reunions brought about by conflict within the fratriarchy is truer to politics than meta-physical existence (which believes in a common good and a common end which transcends the unequal hierarchies of history), or meta-historical existence (which believes in the development of a society without alienation, without privileges, without new schisms, at some time after our present 'pre-history'). We must live with our conflicts as brothers, and not dream of a society, in the present or in the future, which has none. Such a society does not put brotherhood to the test.

Faith and involvement

Involvement is a prestigious – and misleading – word. It is prestigious, because life consists in becoming a witness and an actor instead of being a spectator. The disciples got involved when they took the decision to follow Jesus rather than just watch him pass by. To be a politician is to stop diverting oneself by information in order to act, if possible, without ceasing to be informed. 'Involvement' is the pledge that we give to causes where we have more time, money or heart to lose than reputation to gain. Because politics is divisive, by getting involved we risk leaving one side and becoming inextricably entangled with another, though in fact risk is the spice of life. It demands our trust, asks us to go beyond what we think are our capabilities. Hence the prestige of any involvements in which a person sacrifices his personal security for corporate insecurity. However, the word 'prestige' already indicates that involvement also has its more sinister aspect. Involvement, like almsgiving or prayer, in the Sermon on the Mount, should remain resolutely secret: 'Beware of practising your piety before men in order to be seen by them; for then you will have no reward from your Father who is in heaven. When you give alms, do not let your left hand know what your right hand is doing, so that your alms may be in secret; and your Father who sees in secret will reward you' (Matt. 6.1, 3 f.).

We know that things turn out otherwise. Political involvement is something to be blazoned abroad, publicized, noted, taken advantage of, spread around. It is communicated in good faith, by armband, streamer, petition, subscription, profession. It is as praiseworthy to friends as it is objectionable to enemies. Little by little, those who keep getting involved turn into professionals. The free-lance becomes the partisan. He shuts his ears to anything that might upset his position, and never wearies of singing its praises and commending it. The involved person with a reputation in due course becomes a useful figurehead. Then all that is left is for him to go through a third stage, the most problematical one, when he confuses loyalty with lies, or pragmatism with cynicism, depending on his temperament.

I suppose that this parody of La Bruyère might suggest that it would be better not to become involved, since putting one's heart into something will inevitably bring heartbreak. But those who become involved should know that involvement does not bring salvation. It is simply an attempt at service. There can be no question of having faith in one's involvement, to the point of more or less hallowing the human cause that one serves. In secular political involvement, therefore, the Christian has to remember the demands of spiritual faith, the greatest role of which is, I suppose, to free man from the desire to find salvation in himself or from the thought that he can be saved in another way. The fruits of faith are humility, energy and the strength to look things in the face without being afraid. Faith is afraid of publicity, inertia and illusion. Faith requires spectators to abandon their amateurism and seeks to stop those who are involved from becoming professionals. Faith should not lead us to turn our backs on politics for God's sake or to claim God for our own political party. On the contrary, we need to keep faith with God in our own political involvement, because this faith will make our political life healthier. To turn Matt. 22.21 the other way round: 'Render to God the things that are God's, and to Caesar the things that are Caesar's.'

I would like to quote an extract from a conversation between André Philip and his son-in-law Francis Jeanson, both of whom were very much involved:

'*Jeanson:* You have often seemed to talk as though there were first values, and then the real world in which they had to be incarnated. I do not really understand this kind of chronological privilege which you confer on values over against their embodiment in reality. . .

'*André Philip:* Reality is not just mysterious; it is also chaotic and absurd. I cannot conceive how one can become indignant or complain about the absurdity of reality, because it is normal for it to be absurd until an individual brings order to it. I see no way of moving from reality towards a value judgment. In other words, I am *in* this world, but I am not *of* this world. . . Besides, would it not be better to say "demon" rather than "value"? We live in the midst of demons and fairies. On the one hand there is Father Christmas, and on the other there are class, nation, the proletariat, race, etc., i.e. the "demons" who are part of man's nature and whom he has to judge, discipline and co-ordinate. None of them can be the basis for a value judgment; this value judgment must come from outside, and for me it is a matter of faith.'[43]

Thus faith, which is a judgment coming from outside, does not excuse a man from taking part in the battles he has to fight, but it does keep watch for him against the inevitable demons. It does not lead to the separations of dualism but to the exercise of vigilance. Faith frees him to take part in everything and faith gives love its costly dimension.

Freedom to take part in everything

First of all, faith frees men to play their own part in political choices. I cannot conceive how, in the name of faith, one could put any kind of 'keep out' notice on a political trend or political party which one might otherwise think in all good conscience to be necessary and appropriate in any given situation. There is certainly no such thing as a Christian free market[44] or a Christian free world, Christian socialism or Christian communism, far less any Christian social theory. As a result, it is quite normal that Christians should join together in different groups in support of free enterprise; that there should be 'Christians for Socialism' and 'Christians for Communism'. The church here is a fratriarchy in conflict, consisting of these various communities.

Some people would like the range to be narrower, for example towards the right, on account of the social question and solidarity with the oppressed, or towards the left, on account of materialist ideology, political totalitarianism or atheism. I think that any prohibitions here, however cautiously or skilfully they may be attempted, amount to a manipulation of political life by spiritual life. Faith provides a muzzle instead of a basis for liberty. Faith turns into a scarecrow. It becomes a substitute for ideology and is used to rally forces or to act as a deterrent. It is no longer faith given by God and lived out by man. It is the vehicle for human propaganda which exploits God for its own ends and in order to evade critical judgment, which is the touchstone for any convinced involvement. Everything is allowed. Nothing is forbidden, although nothing is entirely free from hidden demons, nothing is harmless, to take up a fashionable phrase which has often been used more of opponents than of the speaker's own side. We ought to remind ourselves of what St Paul said to the Corinthians who asked him whether they could eat meat sacrificed to idols. Paul gave them complete freedom, but he also advised them not to trouble their brothers' consciences uselessly, if they had yet to learn that to eat such meat was not automatically to be involved in worship of the idols to whom it had been offered (I Cor. 8). Faith brings freedom for eating the political meat that one personally feels can give nourishment to the future of a world society – and that excludes any meat intended merely to defend the interests of a group – while showing oneself at the same time capable of consuming it without recourse to idolatry. I am not understanding idolatry in terms of excess, since certain situations may require excessive solutions, but in terms of the lie which combines clarity about the motes in other peoples' eyes with blindness to the beams in one's own. In more modern language, the idol is ideology, when it abandons its legitimate usefulness to bring about corporate conscientization, and becomes a noxious drug, offering its own kind of salvation. Here, however, rather than feeding on meat, one is getting pseudo-religious intoxication from opium!

I would like to base complete freedom of political choice on faith itself rather than on pluralism. The latter tends to relativize choices to such a degree that it dissipates them in scepticism. It does so even more than tolerance. Tolerance is often no more than politeness, forced and transitory. If faith itself is free, it will act without either terrorism or fascination. It will know that meat is nourishing, but that underlying each kind of meat, at one or other remove, can be found a consuming idol. Thus faith will help us to know that what seems best in theory may in practice produce the worse results, unless people safeguard their spiritual liberty in political involvement. For example, faith will be well aware that liberalism, which in theory is respect for a plurality of initiatives and aspirations, in practice risks engendering an individualistic egotism in private life when times are easy, and producing a competitive jungle when times are hard. In terrifying times (or times of crisis), it can easily turn to fascism. Faith will know equally well that socialism, which in theory is social justice and international solidarity, in practice risks being divided into two varieties: communism, which in the last resort will turn into the socialization of the means of production without social liberties, and a social democracy, which will simply be a market economy with some advantages and correctives provided by socialism. Faith will not be surprised at these setbacks because those who are surprised discover too late that they have been deceived, and never fight back in time. The task of faith is to achieve the freedom to eat meat without swallowing idols. In this respect it plays a healthy part in political work, which always runs the risk of dividing men into fascinated consumers and disgusted non-consumers!

This liberty is not idealistic, but incarnate. I say this as I recall how freely Jesus acted in his life, although that life was lived out under constant pressures and setbacks in a context in which the best (the imminence of the kingdom of God) in fact led to the worst (the cross). However, Jesus was not surprised that things turned out in that way. He did not transform his preaching into an unattainable ideal, nor did he hallow his passion by making it an inevitable destiny. He simply fought as hard as he could, without coming to the bitter conclusion that he had been wrong in the first place. Jesus played his part in political life without swallowing the idol of political success offered to him in his temptation by the devil, the one who introduces a gulf between God's reality and man's. That is why faith, following Jesus and in Jesus, does not topple from the heights of its metaphysical aspirations or its meta-historical pronouncements. Faith does not topple from any height. Its robustness is in keeping with the humility of its knowledge and its involvement in reality. However, we should not turn humility into resignation disguised as modesty. Faith is tenacious. In this respect it resembles the child which constantly falls without doing itself much harm because it is so small and constantly gets up again, for it knows that in spite of all the problems it is made for walking. 'Truly, I say to you, whoever does not receive the kingdom of God like a child shall not enter into it' (Mark 10.15).

Love casts out fear but evokes reverence

When there is this faith, fear disappears, fear of confrontation, fear of having to open one's eyes. Now fear is without doubt the greatest purveyor of hatred and murder. People kill because they are afraid. They take up arms because they suppose that they will soon be attacked, overcome and annihilated. Fear makes men into animals. They become terrifying because they are terrified. They no longer talk, but lurk. They no longer walk, but hunt and keep on their guard. They are no longer open, but hide and put up defences. They no longer participate, but pretend and take advantage. Men are neither violent nor non-violent; they are either confident or afraid.

The simplest definition of love is surely that it is the end of fear. 'There is no fear in love, but perfect love casts out fear. We love, because he first loved us' (I John 4.18f.). God is the one who no longer frightens men because he has taken the first step beyond the vicious circle of suspicion, accusation, condemnation and vengeance. God is love, in that on the cross he puts an end to the confused fear which men have of one another. If his action is to have any significance in our life, then to the eyes of faith, the one who is crucified must not be seen as an idealist, who is impotent even if he is a fellow-sufferer, but as the fullness of God, who is all-powerful and in his action demonstrates that God himself cannot and will not make men fear. To have a political existence under the cross is to seek to overcome in oneself the obscure desire to frighten others. The desire is obscure because it always obstinately pretends that threat comes from the other side. The cross puts an end to the escalation of fear by a possible restoration of confidence and a possible reconstruction of the covenant, which is the social model required of and promised to the fratriarchy in conflict.

However, love should not be understood in idealistic terms as a heady intoxicant which gives place to a rude awakening to reality. Love always risks being the satisfying feeling that we have hearts so large that there is room in them for others. The effect of love is tougher than this stifling embrace. Leibniz gave the simplest definition of it when he wrote, 'Love is to take the point of view and the place of someone else.' So in love, the other person remains who he is, with his resistance, at the very moment when I want to approach him, with my confidence. We have seen this earlier, in the reunions between God and Cain, Abel's murderer; between Esau and Jacob, his deceiver; between Joseph and his eleven brothers, who sold him as a slave; between Jesus and his twelve apostles, who left him in the lurch. These reunions are difficult and hesitant, a mixture of tangible fear and tentative confidence. It is striking how biblical terminology, while banishing fear in the freedom of faith, commends reverence as the beginning of all love and all wisdom towards God and man. The Greek word *phobos*, which should always be translated as 'reverence' and not as 'fear', is for the most part used in the New Testament in a positive sense. For reverence is an awareness that the other person continues to count and to be costly within love, that each moment is astonishment, chance and grace, rather than achievement, triumph and justification. Fear, which isolates, goes away from us, but reverence, which unites, draws close to us.

In political terms, reverence is healthy, when it obliges those in a monopolistic position of power to take their other partners into account. Perhaps the greater reverence now to be found within developed societies, the superpowers, the existing hierarchies, will be salutary if it does not simply turn to fear. In this last quarter of the twentieth century, the threat of nuclear proliferation, the population explosion and the imbalances to which it leads, the deterioration of the environment and ecological concern, the internal disintegration of anything that becomes too big: economies, empires, cities, ideologies, and the suffocation of anything that is too small, family, job, nationalism, culture – concern, reverence for all these problems can lead not only to fear but also to the conflict of love, without involving any metaphysical or meta-historical paradises.

At the centre of faith we find a cross, which rules out self-love by making a place for others, and a resurrection, which opens up the freedom to make use of anything without idolizing it. Faith is not a spiritual deodorant to compensate for and remove the stink of politics. Rather, it is the salt of political life, which should be free from fear, educated by reverence, sustained in an incarnate freedom.

But, someone will say, is faith indispensable? Is it not really superfluous? This question seems to me to be a trap. Some ask it looking for the answer yes, which would disqualify anyone who has no faith but still displays its virtues. Others, who seem to me to be in the majority, put it expecting the answer no, which would absolve everyone from involvement by faith. On the one hand Jesus said to the centurion of Capernaum, a man without faith but yet living by faith: 'Truly, I say to you, not even in Israel have I found such faith' (that is to say, not even among self-confessed Christians) (Matt. 8.10). On the other hand, he also said, 'So every one who acknowledges me before men, I also will acknowledge before my Father who is in heaven' (Matt. 10.32). Faith, then, is not an obligation to do good but the freedom to say that Jesus Christ puts an end to idealism and utopianism by the reality of what God accomplishes, begins and proposes in him, for us, towards us and with us. Faith does not elevate a man spiritually, any more than politics abases God. Faith makes the involvement of Christians in politics healthier: here believers, like all other men and in company with them, find themselves called to banish fear, to practice reverence, and to maintain freedom against the fascination and derision of politics. In this way, spiritual life can prove to be not just an opiate or a sweetener for political life, but leaven, hidden and at work in the dough of human history.

Notes

1. Karl Barth, *The Word of God and the Word of Man*, Hodder 1928, reprinted Harper and Brothers, New York 1957. The text dates from 1922.

2. Rudolf Bultmann, *Jesus and the Word*, Scribner, New York 1934, reprinted Collins 1958. The text dates from 1926.

3. In the bibliography to this chapter I have cited several works to show how interpretation predominates over transcendence from this point on.

4. Here, too, the bibliography will provide some introductory reading to this subject, which I have inevitably had to sketch out very briefly.

5. 'Of making many books there is no end, and much study is a weariness of the flesh' (Ecclesiastes 12.12).

6. I use the word 'economy' in the sense in which it is often to be found in the theology of the Greek Fathers, maintaining the unity of the divine power while emphasizing that its manifestation has been threefold (cf. G. L. Prestige, *God in Patristic Thought*, Heinemann 1936, chapter V).

7. For what follows I am much indebted to an article by Roger Mehl, 'Le fait politique', Centre protestant d'études de Genève, September 1966.

8. Here I draw to a large extent on Hans Walter Wolff, *Anthropology of the Old Testament*, SCM Press and Fortress Press, Philadelphia 1974.

9. 'Brotherhood is a sentiment with which people might feel familiar because they confuse it with human warmth; in fact it has profound depth, and was added almost as an afterthought to the republican slogan, which originally ran "Liberty – equality"' (André Malraux, *Lazare*, NRF, Paris 1974, p. 197).

10. For this quotation, the Hebrew of which is uncertain, I have followed the author's own translation (Tr.).

11. With respects to William Faulkner, *Absalom, Absalom,* Chatto and Windus 1965.

12. Friedrich Engels, 'The Book of the Apocalypse', in Karl Marx and Friedrich Engels, *On Religion,* Progress Publishing House, Moscow 1957.

13. Ernst Käsemann, *New Testament Questions of Today,* SCM Press and Fortress Press, Philadelphia 1969.

14. By 'sevens' I mean the successive episodes in Revelation, where time and again we find a seventh event which has yet to take place.

15. The One is a characteristic of the neo-Platonism of Plotinus. The fall which produces multiplicity brings about separation from the One; purification brings about reunion. When talking about Plato it is better to speak in terms of an ascending dialectic, since Plato never made a complete identification of the One, the Good and the Beautiful in a single sun.

16. 'Society is the complete unity of man with nature – the true resurrection of nature – the accomplished naturalism of man and the accomplished humanism of nature' (Karl Marx, 'Economic and Philosophic Manuscripts of 1844', in Karl Marx and Friedrich Engels, *Collected Works,* Lawrence and Wishart 1975, p. 298).

17. The word 'canonical' signifies that a boundary line has been drawn round certain books: this does not mean that as a result they have become sacred, but rather that they have proved to convey knowledge of God and to hand on the life of his Word. Thus Jews, Christians and Muslims form 'meta-textual' communities. They live with clearly defined canonical texts. That does not, however, mean that they are literalist communities which fail to note the problem presented by the need to move from ancient texts to the present. The canon is what makes this transition necessary.

18. A number of biblical passages certainly have a mythological form and a symbolic meaning. But even these have historical roots and make a hortative point. They do not seek to provide explanations, but to give God a place and to confront man with questions.

19. The metaphysical period of our culture often transformed these sacred texts into Holy Scripture. The critical period, which begins towards the seventeenth century, called attention to their historical and secular character. Does this mean that we must

suppress or diminish their 'holiness', their revolutionary message? That is the context of the present conflict.

20. Immanuel Kant, *Religion within the Limits of Reason Alone*, reprinted Harper and Row, New York 1960.

21. F. Nietzsche, *The Genealogy of Morals*, Second Essay, par. 11, Complete Works XIII, T. N. Foulis, Edinburgh and London 1910, pp.84ff.

22. Above all Gustavo Gutierrez, *Theology of Liberation*, Orbis Books, Maryknoll and SCM Press 1974; Hugo Assmann, *Practical Theology of Liberation*, Search Press 1975; Rubem Alves, *A Theology of Human Hope*, World Publishing, New York 1969 and Anthony Clarke 1975; José Miguez Bonino, *Revolutionary Theology Comes of Age*, SPCK 1975.

23. Cf. above all Jürgen Moltmann, *Theology of Hope*, SCM Press and Harper and Row, New York 1967; *Hope and Planning*, SCM Press and Harper and Row, New York 1971; *The Experiment Hope*, SCM Press and Fortress Press, Philadelphia 1975; Jean-Baptiste Metz, *Theology of the World*, Search Press 1969; also J. Guichard, *Eglise, lutte de classes et stratégies politiques*, Cerf, Paris 1972; Jules Girardi, *Christianisme, libération humaine, lutte des classes*, Cerf, Paris 1972. However, the last two authors are closer to the Latin Americans than to the Germans.

24. Karl Marx, 'Contribution to the Critique of Hegel's Philosophy of Law', in Karl Marx and Friedrich Engels, *Collected Works*, Lawrence and Wishart 1975, p.175.

25. Here Moltmann uses the German word *Entaüsserung*, a classical term from Hegelianism and Marxism. In Hegel it means alienation in a positive sense, i.e. a kind of stripping of oneself which also leads to enrichment; in Marxism it means alienation in a negative sense: dispossession of oneself, the impoverishment of the exploited for the gain of the exploiters. Moltmann gives the word quite a different sense: it is to exteriorize oneself through hope and expectation. Exteriorization is hope, whereas for Hegel alienation is the necessary entry into negativity and for Marx the destructive experience of privation. (For the English reader, the situation is further complicated by the fact that the English translation of *Theology of Hope* translates this vital word as 'expend'. Tr.)

26. Jürgen Moltmann, *Theology of Hope*, pp.337f.; cf. id., *The Crucified God*, SCM Press and Harper and Row, New York 1974; Jean-Baptiste Metz, *Befreiendes Gedachtnis*, Jesus-Christi, Mainz 1970.

27. Henri Desroche, *Sociologie de l'espérance*, Calmann-Lévy Paris 1973. Georges Crespy has clearly shown in his last article that Christianity cannot be seen as a development from deluded messianic expectations, as in Loisy's famous remark: 'Jesus looked for the kingdom of God and the church came.' It is, rather, the realization of messianic expectations along the lines of the happy formula: 'Jesus announced the kingdom of God and his resurrection took place' (Georges Crespy, *Etudes théologiques et religieuses* 2, Montpellier 1976, p.210).

28. René Marlé, *La singularité chrétienne*, Casterman 1970.

29. It is remarkable to see the reappearance of the word redemption and not just liberation among the philosophers of the Frankfurt school, though they have no theological concern. Thus Adorno ends his *minima moralia*: 'The only philosophy which could stand fast in the face of despair would be an attempt to consider things as they present themselves from the point of view of redemption. The only light of knowledge is that which redemption casts on the world: all the rest is obscured by reconstructions and remains a matter of technique' (quoted on the cover of *Utopie, marxisme selon Ernst Bloch*, Payot, Paris 1976).

30. Jürgen Moltmann, *The Crucified God*, p.249.

31. An allusion to the heresy of Noetus, which was condemned about AD 200. Noetus believed that there was only one God, the Father, who was born, suffered and died; for if Christ is God, he is surely the Father, otherwise he would not be God; and if Christ suffered, God suffered, for he is a unity.

32. Karl Marx, 'Economic and Philosophic Manuscripts of 1844', in Karl Marx and Friedrich Engels, *Collected Works* 3, Lawrence and Wishart 1975, pp.336, 302. Having said this, I shall not enter into the dispute as to which is the more Marxist of the two Marxs, in which the young Marx is favoured by Michel Henry and the old Marx by Louis Althuiser. I do, however, think that the preference for materialism over against naturalism which has been an almost constant feature of Marx and Marxism from a fairly early stage has encumbered what could otherwise have been rigorous thought with an unscientific dualism which has given rise to unconvincing scholasticism and unconvincing apologetic.

33. Karl Marx, 'The Circular against Kriege', quoted by Henri Desroche, *Socialisme et sociologie religieuse*, Cujas, Paris 1965, p.329.

34. Karl Marx, *The Class Struggles in France* (*1843–1850*), Martin Lawrence 1934, p.44.

35. In his 1523 treatise, 'On Temporal Authority and the Limits of the Obedience owed to it', Luther discusses the necessity for the use of the sword, pressures in the temporal domain and its utter harmfulness in the spiritual domain. For 'Christians of their own accord and without constraint do what is good, and in that respect the Word of God is enough for them.' This is the beginning of the so-called 'doctrine of the two kingdoms'.

36. For all this, see Konrad Lorenz, *On Aggression*, Methuen 1966. Unfortunately, by his exaggerated stress on the involvement of man in the animal world, Lorenz fails to note sufficiently the substitution of cultural and juridical rules for natural and biological instincts.

37. R. H. Tawney, *Religion and the Rise of Capitalism* (1922), reprinted Penguin Books 1938, pp.34f.

38. *Encyclical letter of . . . Leo XIII on the Condition of Labour*, official translation, Westminster Press, London 1891, pp.11f.

39. Valéry Giscard d'Estaing, *Démocratie française*, Fayard 1976, p.56.

40. Karl Marx, *Contribution to the Critique of Political Economy*, (1857), my translation.

41. Antonio Gramsci, *La construction du parti communiste* (*1923–1926*), Einaudi, Turin 1971, p.13.

42. Karl Marx, 'The Idealist View of History', from *The Holy Family*, in Karl Marx, *Selected Writings*, ed. David McLellan, OUP 1977, p.139.

43. André Philip, *André Philip par lui-même ou les voies de la liberté*, Aubier, Paris 1971, p.250.

44. At this point I am deliberately avoiding the word capitalism for two reasons. The first is technical: any society (no matter whether it is free market or has central planning) must levy a certain capital from labour for the financing of its investments. The second, and chief reason, is emotional: capitalism, like totalitarianism, has become a symbol of evil which hampers reflection and action with respect to it.

Bibliography

The subjects I have touched on are vast, and this book is a short one. This bibliography offers suggestions for further reading in connection with each chapter. I have included a number of novels, so that there is stimulus for the imagination as well as the intellect.

1. The Nature of Politics and the Mission of the Church

Barth, Karl, *The Word of God and the Word of Man*, Hodder 1928, reprinted Harper and Brothers, New York 1957
'The Christian Community and the Civil Community', in *Against the Stream*, SCM Press 1954, pp.13–50

Bultmann, Rudolf, *Jesus Christ and Mythology*, Scribner, New York and SCM Press 1960

Delumeau, Jean, *Le christianisme va-t-il mourir?*, Hachette, Paris 1977

Ebeling, Gerhard, *The Nature of Faith*, Collins 1961

Freund, Julien, *L'essence du politique*, Sirey, Paris 1965

Marlé, René, *Parler de Dieu aujourd'hui. La théologie herméneutique d'Ebeling*, Cerf, Paris 1975

Metz, Jean-Baptiste, *Theology of the World*, Search Press 1969

Moltmann, Jürgen, *Theology of Hope*, SCM Press and Harper and Row, New York 1967

Nietzsche, Friedrich, 'The Anti-Christ', in *Twilight of the Idols*, Penguin Books 1969

Prigent, Pierre, *Flash sur l'Apocalypse*, Delachaux, Neuchâtel–Paris 1974

Ricoeur, Paul, *Le conflit des interprétations. Essais d'herméneutique*, Seuil, Paris 1975

Weil, Eric, *Philosophie politique*, Vrin, Paris 1956

Xhaufflaire, M., *La 'théologie politique'. Introduction à J.-B. Metz*, Cerf, Paris 1972

Zahrnt, Heinz, *The Question of God. Protestant Theology in the Twentieth Century*, Collins 1969

2. Biblical Foundations in the Prophets and Apostles

Cabries, Jean, *Saint Jacob*, Livre de poche, no.3174
Faulkner, William, *Absalom, Absalom*, Chatto and Windus 1965
Jeremias, Joachim, *Jerusalem in the Time of Jesus*, SCM Press and Fortress Press, Philadelphia 1969
Käsemann, Ernst, *New Testament Questions of Today*, SCM Press and Fortress Press, Philadelphia 1969
Marx, Karl and Engels, Friedrich, *On Religion*, Progress Publishing House, Moscow 1957
Mury, Gilbert, *Christianisme primitif et monde moderne*, La Palatine, Paris 1966
Rad, Gerhard von, *Old Testament Theology*, reprinted SCM Press 1975
Steinbeck, John, *East of Eden*, Heinemann 1968
Wolff, Hans Walter, *Anthropology of the Old Testament*, SCM Press and Fortress Press, Philadelphia 1974

3. Relating the Bible to Contemporary Situations

Charpentier, Etienne, *Des évangiles à l'Evangile*, Croire et comprendre, Le Centurion, Paris 1976
Dartigues, André, *Le croyant devant la critique moderne*, Croire et comprendre, Le Centurion, Paris 1975
George, A., and Grelot, P. (eds.), *Introduction à la Bible. Le Nouveau Testament*, Desclée, Paris 1976–1977
Ladrière, Jean, *L'articulation du sens*, Aubier/Cerf/Delachaux/ Desclée 1970
Spinoza, Benedict de, 'Tractatus Theologico-politicus', in *Political Works*, ed. A. G. Wernham, OUP 1958
Wolff, Hans Walter, *Ancien Testament. Problèmes d'introduction*, Labor et Fides, Geneva 1973

4. Words and Violence

Chabrol, Jean-Pierre, *Les fous de Dieu*, Folio 257, Gallimard, Paris 1970

Cullmann, Oscar, *The State in the New Testament*, SCM Press 1956
Ellul, Jacques, *Violence*, Seabury Press, New York 1969 and SCM Press 1970
Hegel, G. W. F., *The Phenomenology of Mind*, Allen and Unwin 1931
Kant, Immanuel, *Religion within the Limits of Reason Alone*, reprinted Harper and Row, New York 1960
Leenhardt, Franz, *Le chrétien doit-il servir l'Etat?*, Labor et Fides, Geneva 1939
Ricoeur, Paul, *Histoire et vérité*, Seuil, Paris 1964
Secretan, P., *Vérité et pouvoir*, L'âge de l'homme, Lausanne 1970
A la recherche d'une théologie de la violence, with contributions by P. Blanquart, L. Beinaert, P. Dabezies, A. Dumas, Casamayor, P. Lecocq, Cerf, Paris 1968

5. From the Promise of the Resurrection to the Memory of the Cross

Alves, Rubem, *A Theology of Human Hope*, World Publishing, New York 1969 and Anthony Clarke 1975
Bloch, Ernst, *Das Prinzip Hoffnung*, Berlin 1959
Comblin, J., *Théologie de la révolution*, Editions Universitaires, Paris 1970
Desroche, Henri, *Sociologie de l'espérance*, Calmann-Lévy, Paris 1973
Moltmann, Jürgen, *Theology of Hope*, SCM Press and Harper and Row, New York 1967
Gutierrez, Gustavo, *Theology of Liberation*, Orbis Books, Maryknoll and SCM Press 1974
Discussion sur la théologie de la révolution, with contributions by Jürgen Moltmann, Dom Helder Camara, H. Gollwitzer, A. Rich, H. Assmann et al., Cerf/Mame, Paris 1972
Croyants hors frontières, with contributions by G. Casalis, M.-M. Davy, P. Gallay, L. Hurbon, V. Paques and M. Sinda, Buchet-Chastel, Paris 1975
Théologies de la libération en Amérique latine (with bibliography), with contributions by Jean-Marie Aubert, Julien Freund, Eduardo Ibarra, J. von Nieuwenhove and Marc Michel, Le Point théologique 10, Beauchesne 1974

6. Spiritual Life and Politics

Aragon, L., *Les beaux quartiers*, Folio 241, Gallimard, Paris 1970

Bieler, André, *Le développement fou*, Centurion, Paris and Labor et Fides, Geneva 1973

Biot, François, *Théologie du politique*, Editions Universitaires, Paris 1972

Coste, René, *Analyse marxiste et foi chrétienne*, Editions Ouvrières, Paris 1976

Desroche, Henri, *Marxisme et religions*, Presses universitaires de France, Paris 1962

Girardi, Jules, *Christianisme, libération humaine, lutte des classes*, Cerf, Paris 1973

Gollwitzer, Helmut, *Christian Faith and the Marxist Criticism of Religion*, St Andrew Press 1970

Guichard, Jean, *Eglise, luttes des classes et stratégies politiques*, Cerf, Paris 1972

London, Artur, *L'aveu*, Folio 13, Gallimard, Paris 1969

Philip, André, *André Philip par lui-même ou les voies de la liberté*, Aubier, Paris 1971

Pury, Roland de, *Présence de l'éternité*, Delachaux, Neuchâtel–Paris 1943

Simon, René, *Fonder la morale*, Seuil, Paris 1974

Wiechert, E., *Missa sine nomine*, Livre de poche 1506

Eglise et société économique. L'enseignement social des papes de Léon XIII à Pie XIII, ed. J.-Y. Calvez and J. Perrin, Aubier, Paris 1959